Astral Philosophy

How To Connect To Your Inner Light And Higher Self

By

Lucy Caxton Brown

Published by New Generation Publishing in 2019

First Edition

www.newgeneration-publishing.com

Cover; The Sun; After a Painting by Geraldine Bridgewater

Contents

Letter to reader, ... 1
Chapter One AWAKE! 5
Chapter Two CREATE 11
Chapter Three PRACTICE MAKES PERFECT 18
Chapter Four THE LIGHT KINGDOM 26
Chapter Five MIND AND SOUL 35
Chapter Six THE LIGHT WITHIN YOU 48
Chapter Seven YOUR ASTRAL SELF 56
Further Reading 76

Poems

Awake	Lucy Caxton Brown	6
Unclouded Ray	Anon	7
The Panorama of the Mind	Thomas South	10
The Mind	Lucy Caxton Brown	11
When Two Become One (1)	Lucy Caxton Brown	16
For All the Day	Shakespeare	37
The Beauty	Alexander Pushkin	41
Divine Well-being	Lucy Caxton Brown	43
The Light Within	Lucy Caxton Brown	55
When Two Become One	Lucy Caxton Brown	69
New	Lucy Caxton Brown	70

Dear Reader,

Many people realize that they have a soul and that when the body dies the soul continues to exist. In other words the soul is immortal. But what people will find hard to understand is that not only does the soul live on but so too does the mind and the personality. The body will die but the soul will not. The brain will die but the mind and personality will not die. You continue to be aware long after your brain and body have died.

As individuals, we think about ourselves and our life in terms of time limited achievements. We have concentrated on the material development of our lives and ignored our spiritual self. We think in terms of physical birth and physical death being the beginning and end of our life. But our soul was already alive before we were born and will continue to exist after we die. We had memories of other lives before we were born and we came down here to learn by being emotionally tested on the material plane of existence.

These days many people know more about what happens to us after death than at any other time in our history. People are actively sharing their near death, out of body, and after death experiences and technology is providing intriguing evidence that there are indeed other dimensions of awareness where we continue to be who we have always been, simply put, our soul-self. Perhaps the ancient hermetic search for the 'Holy Grail' and the practice of the 'Great Work' in Medieval and later in Victorian times, by mystics and philosophers, writers and theologians, was the process of searching for the hidden and holiest part of ourselves.

This hidden knowledge is not new, though it has been lost for many centuries. When the Bible says; God made man in his own image, that image was not the physical body tempted by sinful lust and prone to imperfection. No, the image spoken of was, so I believe, the immortal soul and mind that is within each and everyone of us.

It is our own Astral soul and mind and it is living and communicating within us even now as I write this to you.

Once we acknowledge the eternal existence of our soul and mind we will naturally want to develop a process from which we can learn all about who we are. We will begin to benefit from the astral knowledge and be awarded abilities that only it can bestow upon us within this terrestrial life.

As Astral beings we may then go on to make a significant

contribution towards astral development within the field of human psychic consciousness on this our beautiful terrestrial planet called Earth.

Time is of the essence because although we have developed physically and significantly on the material plane of activity we are at a difficult point in our history as we enter upon the threshold of human beings becoming artificially mechanized. It will mean that our feelings and thoughts and our very existence can be programmed and manipulated by technology.

I cannot bare to think of the possibility that one day our mind and soul, divine astral beings, could be locked up in a synthetic and remotely controlled body. We may be unable to express ourselves totally because the natural interconnected tissues of our body, through which our mind and soul manifest, will be replaced or adjusted in order to take full advantage of the latest artificial intelligence technology.

Relationships with other humans, animals, and plant life may become fraught with difficulty as we drive relentlessly forward in our demand for physical perfection. Indeed it is likely that we will take full advantage of the ability to manufacture soulless life, robots to entertain, serve and feed us and even to have relationships with! It means the individual capable of academic or mystical thought may become a rare anomaly. Something to be erased out of existence.

Naturally I think this is a worrying phenomena in our development. I suppose it is only natural that we will want a better life and so expect that technological advancements will give us every opportunity to succeed and be free of disease and pain. There is no doubt that this can be a good thing but if it comes at the cost of our understanding that first and foremost we are spiritual beings, then we risk losing the very essence of our being and the promise of eternal life which is most certainly part of what I call the 'Divine Plan'.

If we want to evolve within this lifetime we should know our full story and who we really are. We should be able to connect to our soul, which is not the body, and understand how our mind, which is not the brain, operates and feels. I want to help open the shut palaces of the mind so that we can take important steps towards returning to the original design of a divine being. The being we were before what is commonly referred to as the 'Fall'.

If we know the way our mind works and the benefits and hardships it can give us, does it not also make sense to know our soul, how it operates and our spirit, how it energises?

Let us give thanks that the knowledge that has been denied can be revealed to us who must now work diligently to learn all about our Astral being.

I know that some find that going inside their mind can be an uncomfortable experience or place to be. It is another reason why I have written this book, in the hope that the verses will help to improve our experiences of spirituality. But some home truths must be welcomed if we are to make the effort and be rewarded with new abilities.

None of us are perfect. If we were we wouldn't be here in the first place! But clearly we can become more perfect and when we do the Astral plane rewards us. I'm not going to speak of these rewards now but you will become aware of them as you read this book. I promise you they are manifold and include everything you would personally want for yourself.

'Astral Philosophy' aims to help every reader find their personal pathway to their divine self.

The soul, spirit and mind, who reads the words in this book should be able to achieve a meaningful level of coordination, awareness and knowledge, through the gentle absorption of these philosophical truths. You may find the language flowery on occasions, I am a poet after all! I hope it's timelessness and beauty will connect to the deeper recesses of being where the mind and soul are to be found.

This book can be read several times. As your understanding expands so the meaning of my words will grow. Do not rush the process.

There are no prizes given for reading it quickly. You cannot learn what I have to teach rapidly. We must all grow into the spiritual process of evolvement and this naturally takes time. Some of you will find it easy, others not so easy. Please do not measure your performance in one area as a reason to have automatic success in other areas. We all have our individual path to follow before we become adept.

You will become aware that in the following pages a new philosophy starts to take shape. A philosophy that if accepted, could unite all religions of the world. Imagine a peaceful world with no more wars. Imagine a disease free planet. All of this is possible if only enough people can become less fearful and more confident in themselves. They will understand that it is an existence of eternal being where death is no longer considered the end of life.

I have developed my understanding through years of reading, research, and personal experience. I do not say I am an expert by any means. But I do have this knowledge that I wish to share with you. Let me say I am still learning myself and this is the first book in a series that I will write providing I continue to progress.

Despite some very unhappy episodes in my life, and some I have found hard to accept, I am now and always will be a very happy person. Happy because I have met my soul and seen the divine light within. That divine light is within you too and I will teach you how to see it.

I have told my friends about the 'midnight sun' as I like to call it, and how it has guided me and my work and now I present all that I have discovered and experienced so that you may open your door to self-knowledge. Take your time and I hope you enjoy the process of learning about your Astral self.

Lucy

Chapter One

AWAKE!

If you want a supreme state of consciousness do this. When you are asleep be aware of what you are dreaming and wonder why you dreamt it. Learn from it. Awake!

In our dreams we are able to communicate with each other in ways that cannot easily be explained unless one discusses the phenomena in a spiritual way. Each of us has the memory of an ancient soul lurking within and just waiting to be known. No matter how spiritually blind a person may be or unwilling to recognise their own shortcomings, dreams invariably depict their failings honestly and contain metaphors designed to prod them gently into a state of greater self-awareness. There is no doubt that dreams provide a great learning experience. Try to remember them when you awake. Learn from them. Your soul quite likely speaks to you in your dreams.

Our minds can and do change the world. If we would let them see the beauty we would lose fear and build heaven rather than hell. Perform what is right because it is right to do so. Virtue is its own reward.

One spiritual eye is worth a thousand physical eyes, actually the number is meaningless. It could so easily be a million or ten billion!

Your soul is illuminated by a light which sees all things. The truth therein and the truth that is in itself. If you search yourself you will see the light and know it is part of you that will never die. Shut your eyes then open your inner eye and look at what you see. Wait for the light to shine. It will shine for you one evening. Then all your dreams will come true.

Stand in the clear sphere of your being. There in the midst of 'High Heaven' face the spiritual sun or look through the third eye of mind and search for the light that mind alone can see. Here is some ancient knowledge that was lost to us but spoken of in the monuments of Egypt, Greece, and Rome, and by their ancient philosophers and writers.

It may benefit you to consider the meaning of these philosophers words;

'All things may be the objects of our hope since nothing hopeless anywhere is found. All things with ease Divinity effects and naught can frustrate his almighty power.' *Lirius*

'The fear of death renders a man sad through the ignorance of his soul, therefore recognise what God is, and what there is in you, that recognises God.' *Sextus the Pythagorean*

'Is it the Gods who put this fire in our minds or is it that each man's relentless longing becomes a God to him?' *Euryalus*

'The sun is the eye and soul of things which have a natural subsistence. For through it all things become visible, are generated and rise into existence.' *Archytas*

'If the soul at death passes into the state of being dead, and if there is no return journey, the stock of souls must finally be exhausted and life on earth would come to an end.' *Phaedo*

'The creation of a new soul out of nothing is not possible.' *Plato*

'You have in yourself something similar to God and therefore use yourself as the Temple of God on account of that which is in you resembles God.' *Sextus the Pythagorean.*

It is better to fail at something important than to succeed at something unimportant! The soul is energised intellectually so think good things with your mind. It is by the removal of the primal veil that the great secret of the self is revealed. The human body has within and without an etheric vital body and a divine soul body.

The creation of a soul is a divine practice, in other words, God creates souls. Music has the power to harmonise and transform the individual.

Watch for the reflected light within and wherever you see it admire it and love it for without it you do not exist.

It is a sad fact today that there is such a lamentable departure of the divine in humans. Divinity came long before religion.

We only live in a small part of ourselves. When we wake up we find there is so much more to the world and us.

Awake

I hope that you may be found and find
That you may be known and know
That you may be healed and heal
That you may be loved and give love
Meditate on the words and
Partake in the revelation to come
Your mind will interpret the words as it sees fit and
As it grows it will see even more meaning

The words will help your mind expand it's awareness
Awake soul of mine
Awake and see the divine
Awake soul of mine and
Make this earthly body sublime
Who knows their own mind?
Who knows their soul?
Who knows about the Spirit?
They who know the mind and soul
Know also the spirit and if they know all this
They are on the path towards perfection
To know this is to 'Know Thyself'
To truly know thyself is to know the divine part of ourselves

God put intelligence in the soul and the soul in the body. The soul circles around upon itself. The soul is invisible to physical eyes and it is divine. It carries with it full consciousness.

It is by the thought of the Universal Mind that the world soul is brought into being . By raising our awareness into the heart of our soul, we raise ourselves up closer to divinity and closer to God, so that we may partake and receive that greater divinity from God. The divine in our soul is the divine in the universe. We have to realise the truth by getting rid of the ignorance which hides it from us.

Where shines eternal God's unclouded ray
And guilds the realms of intellectual day
For this my golden harp, with art divine
Has told Plotinus, bliss is thine!

Anon

Listen to the quiet voice of the soul and soon you will hear an opera.

We possess such things that are of the greatest divinity and yet millions of people never think of the treasures they have within themselves so focused are they on what others think of them. It is a sign of our culture that needs amending.

We are not only bodies but winged souls. In all this world nothing can keep its shape . All things are born to change, but a soul is a soul. It comes to the body as a live soul and it leaves the body as a live soul.

Every form hastens into a sameness with itself. The soul establishes an image of herself in the body. The soul contains regenerative powers and the soul when it leaves the body of life remembers all the lives it has lived. Know thyself, know thy soul and what it is capable of.

Practice makes perfect. Develop your inner sight, and see the light within. Light sees light and when it beholds itself it feels good and you awake knowing something is inside of you that is the real divine you. Receive the light become one with the light.

The power lies within each one of us, the treasure of all treasures. 'The Manna of Heaven, the source of all spiritual nourishment is within you.' Jesus said it!

Without light there is nothing therefore in essence we too are light. Through light, mind and soul pushes itself into matter. To see the light within ourselves is to understand the creation principle where everything is possible.

Many have endeavoured to make use of the secret knowledge of wise people of ancient origin , to know what they knew and to be able to accomplish it. The day is not far when the truth will be revealed and we will all be free to accomplish it. Amen to that.

The first step is to understand how light can be separated from the darkness. Astral gold from the rays of the sun. The spirit cannot light up the body unless the soul is active. So activate your soul. See the light. I am not speaking metaphorically. The inner light exists you just need to learn how to see it. I am teaching you. Have faith and you will see it.

The spirit can transform the soul, by having a mind to, a willingness to, and then the divine thoughts well up. So to the eyes of the soul I say , search, find, and look at the inner light with your picture making mind.

Since the Kingdom of Heaven is within you, the mountain of God makes us all dwellers on the threshold seeking experiences that lie beyond the common field of consciousness.

Friend if God elects you to this art, he will in time, bestow the knowledge of it, the search for the power of the soul in humanity, or how God really wanted us to experience life at this stage of our evolution.

How does Christ become flesh again? Christ becomes flesh within you the human. Arise, awaken, knock and the door will be opened. The soul must desire. Ask and it shall be given.

May the rays of light reach you without refraction, the work of will power in it's redirections not outwards but inwards. There lies true exploration and true discovery my dear friend.

'Our tendency to fragment the world and ignore the dynamic interconnectedness of all things is responsible for many of our problems. Our current way of fragmenting the world into parts not only doesn't work but may even lead to our extinction.' *David Bohm*

Apocalypse is the new heaven and the new earth declared within us. Light attracts light. So see the light and you will get more light. Unless we learn how to overcome all fragmentation nationally, religiously, and culturally, we are always going to be at war. It is possible to overcome war so let us do it now.

How much more pleasing it is to be surrounded by love rather than hate. We are truly the makers of our own reality and eternity is a long time to be happy in. End the war. The meaning of true power is compassion, empathy, virtue, and self control.

The Quest for the Grail is a task that lies before all who seek the hidden and divine wisdom. Now become the sacred vessel into which the divine wine of inspiration is to be poured. Prepare yourself profoundly my sincere friend. The Grail represents the loftiest of spiritual realities that remain mostly hidden today. To raise up a magical instrument or holy cup is to bring about the manifestation of your own spiritual reality and activate it within you so that it becomes operational.

Whom does the Grail serve? It nourishes those that try, those that love and serve humanity, serve God, serve the Grail and serve yourself! The cosmic climate offers more than just a ray of hope. There is magic in the air. Believe and let it happen for you. You who elevate the Grail in solemn ritual are making an offering of yourself so far as it is possible, as a receiver for divine power to flow through you for the benefit of the whole of humanity. Ultimately the truth will come to you from within. The spirit can transform the soul. Learn to turn it on.

Try to do that today. God fabricated the mind and willed both for the glory of God and our benefit, that God's works should be understood by us, so be not afraid to enquire in all sincerity into the workings of mind. God knows your reasons better than you and will reward you accordingly.

The panorama of the mind, the pan,
The all in all, the great in little man,
These are a little spice of what you may
Expect if you will look in sir one day
And yet which few , comparatively few,
Still have believed but not known what to do
Or say upon a subject yet too new
To be received as orthodox and true

Thomas South

If you hear me knocking let me in. Nothing is hidden that will not manifest. Welcome to the world of Mind and to your mind in particular! The reign of mind is about to commence on Earth. This is the 'New Jerusalem'. To those that overcome will I give to eat of the hidden manna and I will give a white stone and in the stone a new name written, which no one knows except the person that receives it.

Light gives form. Light expands and contracts. Light of light, spirit light, All that is hidden will be found. Welcome to the power of your mind and the power of the 'Universal Mind'. Watch as you begin to make the connections.

A reality is a construct of mind. Our minds watch and partake of boundless, infinite Universal Mind. There is no reality apart from that which is created by the integration of mind thoughts. We create our own reality. Brain does not create consciousness. Mind creates the brain.

We live in a universe that we are just beginning to understand and it is not out there, but within. Reality is established by interaction of consciousness with its environment the visibility of which may or may not be perceived or understood.

Did you know that your mind is working hard to teach you important lessons? Lessons that in your awake state you are unaware of. That is why I say wake up! Wake up to the offer of miracles that impress upon us our true abilities to love and heal. Awake now!

Chapter Two

CREATE

Through nature draw out your soul and activate its power. Watch the light rays beam across the ether of your mind. Multiply the light rays and expand the light rays in your mind. This is real work. How else will you develop? Do not be disappointed or feel you have failed ever. You must know that the inner light of which I speak does not always show itself. You must persevere. Don't give up. Then watch the bright colours, the neon lights and listen to the songs of the mind.

The father reveals himself through the son, the mother through the daughter, and God through all during the hymns of the mind. The fear of God and the respect of God is the beginning of all wisdom. Open the door yourself to higher conscious awareness.

From within and from without search for the Divine Presence whereabouts. There is a fluid of divine vitalising energy that permeates everything and is resident even in the air we breathe. So remember to breathe deeply as you go through your day and allow your bare feet to touch the Earth. Blessings to you all.

When I speak of the Mind
I do not mean the brain
So get that firmly into your head
I know enough to hold my tongue
But not enough to speak!
What I have found commands silence
And that is why I write instead
To you my very dear friend

By God, through nature, draw out your soul and activate the power. Let holy alchemy de-compound the images with the inner eye and introverted light , Into a veiled ethereal world of no sense but much being!

Materially, all is defined by specific consciousness and a gravitational field but not the spiritual. Everything rises or falls in a vacuum by its own energised chord. If you understand me it is a life changer.

You are now in the world of visible thought so time has no actual meaning for you here. When you see the inner sun that I have spoken of you are newly baptised in a celestial divine fountain.

I will show you things you have never seen before so keep seeing the sun of your inner soul as I have showed you. It will nurture your soul bring it to more life for it is magical nurturing and creative. It is vital for you.

The 'Golden Light of Life' returns after some 1900 years of bereft and beleaguered power. It now returns as a personal light for you bearing vital power of divine magnitude. You are now witnessing it's birth within your own sacred body. Congratulations.

That 'Golden Light of Life ' that resides within us all, that eternal and internal light that has always been demands recognition from you now. Protect it and it will protect you.

As *Hermes Trismegistus* says, 'My Sol, *(inner sun of the soul)* my beams, are most inward and secretly in me. My own Luna is also my light, exceeding every light, and my good things are better than all other good things. I give freely and reward the intelligent with joy, gladness, glory, riches and delight, and them that seek after me, I make to know and understand and to possess divine things.'

Let us be clear. The mind is not in the brain it is in all of you. By light, the invisible becomes visible. The door is opened when the male and female creative spirits *(an inner sun and an inner moon)* rise together. Then you will have an inestimable treasure. What can this mean spiritually? The moon reflects light from the sun. The sun light illuminates and gives waves of electromagnetic radiation in different spectrum's. Infrared, X-rays, ultraviolet light, radio waves and neutrinos to name a few.

Here on earth that light energy is converted into chemical energy and forms the basis for life to exist.

The divine gift is received spontaneously by nature and not by being clever. You must watch for the awakening of your universal light , that midnight sun that I speak of, (I call it the midnight sun because you can see it best between the hours of midnight and 4 am) within the treasury of your own universal nature. It is the living gold from which you can spread light and life within you.

In the treasury of your universal nature, watch for the awakening of it's objective light, it is the living gold. Now the key to the Philosopher's Stone, is to learn how to work the internal light of yours. Learn to build and project the celestial light.

Why should anyone be interested in self-discovery when there is so much to occupy and distract themselves with? The answer is because whatever is out there will end up within you as a memory. But to master your destiny is to live life to the full.

It is often said about money, that you might as well spend now as you cannot take it with you when you die. But if you really knew how much of yourself you will take with you, you will make improvements to your being for your future happiness.

The greatest things or secrets of life cannot be seen, so it is pointless searching the physical realms for them. This is what the philosopher poet knows and the non-believer does not.

When our collective beliefs and emotions become a concert of psychic projection a doorway between this world and the Astral plane opens. When we pray for peace and love together we open the door. The same with fear when we feel it we breed it!

Because scientists have not seen soul and spirit they say they do not exist. Yet there is plenty they have not seen that exists and plenty that they think they have seen , that does not exist!

The work I speak of is both to be done within us and around us and can be started in the day or the night with eyes shut or eyes open. Wisdom and faith are the instigators, selflessness and patience the mitigators. The sooner you start the better for you.

Through all of our life we ask the question, Why? It doesn't matter where on earth we come from or what our culture is, the question 'Why ' requires an answer. The answer is to be found within. My writings will teach you how to find your answer.

We instinctively know that there is much more to our soul's journey than we are experiencing in this life. We know something is missing from our life and we know we must find it. That is why the question, why am I hear is always on our minds. I will help you find it if you let me.

You are a self renewing spirit, A soul with magnetic virtues. Know that a great veil opaquely protects the timeless and divine mystery that hangs before all. Though it has remained hidden for centuries by the seal of God, you can open it and change your life.

Using this knowledge try and open the shut palaces of your mind. Remember the mind operates through the body and the brain and all matter. A pure mind becomes saturated with the divine light and receives the virtue of some wonderful effects.

Some say they can't awaken the creative potential of their mind without being controlled by the mechanical aspects of thoughts and desires. The best way to do this is to imagine you are at a cinema. At first the screen is blank then pictures form.

Divinisation! What a wonderful concept. Wisdom the science of truth is in us all. Self knowledge is a way to know the truth of universal nature. Ascend in your thought and visualise the light that I speak of. It is your own personal sun that shines for you at night.

Slowly the change is manifest in you as you open the shut palaces of the mind. Use your inner eye to follow the light, the midnight sun, to your native land, peering as you do, through a glass darkly. Then perceive the light that comes from Spirit.

It takes time to open the shut palaces of the mind. Make no mistake you are making great progress as you search for the rays of the universal light, The light I call your own sun. The light of your soul. The mind of power seeks the mind of light and is always happy to do so.

Searching through the universal ray of light that comes from Spirit. You will shortly find the eye of heaven, an eye at the heart of darkness. Seek it, Look at it, let it see you , look into that eye buried within mind with all of the honesty, truth and love that you possess.

My dear friend, Though we have not met, I feel I know you well. Now find that hidden spark that lays concealed within you. Once found it becomes a flame of knowing. Learn to listen to the silent voice within you. A flame of knowledge. You will become a star and only have to shine to give light to the darkness.

'The fruit which I have brought forth is the sun.' *(written on the great Temple at Suis)*

Your sun is the centre of your galaxy, your mind a galaxy of intuition, the fire-spirit of life. Sacro-sancto the star fire of nature and the supernatural centre of every living being.

I speak of that true light that lights every person that comes into the world. The eye of mind must no longer just work outwardly but turn itself inside and intellectually energise and generate divine light within the mind and soul.

So away with the body and the brain and on with the real business at hand. There is so much more to your life remaining to be discovered and there is only one way to truly know yourself, mind, body and soul. You have to travel within and I will show you how if you agree.

Now my friend, What does the midnight sun show us? The mind is a galaxy of intuition and a tapestry of celestial colours upon which angels draw their moments in time. Spirits of the light levitate and dance to entrance you. All is thought as the various forms appear. But try not to let it be your thought. Let the forms appear as they want to not as you will. Watch as the future unfolds for you without trying to harness its powers to do your will.

The eyes of truth are always watching over you. Those who understand everything but lack knowledge of themselves know nothing! There is a perfect light at the heart of a person of light. The sun shines for us all.

Certainly survival is on a lot of people's minds. Experiences that are not properly understood and let go of work in the mind as a virus with a snowballing effect to produce growing discontent of the ego. The solution is to love your enemy and be patient.

You are the perfect day and the perfect night. In you dwells the sun that never sets.

Once seen it can never be forgotten because it illuminates the Spirit and awakens the eyes of the soul.

I speak of the power that is hidden in every person. Hidden so that to find it, you must actively search. Sacro-sancto the fire spirit of life and the supernatural centre of every living being. You shall want for nothing when you discover it.

Daily exercise your intellect intelligently and energetically. Activate the pineal gland. Visions are mental because the mind sees with the eyes of the soul and the spirit. When you think, think deeply, wisely, honestly and in deep respect of the light that you now grow within your being.

The hand that moves us is divine. The light within you divine and once seen will activate a sublime change that will last forever if you work with it. In the temple that is your soul see the light emanating from your mind watch it dance before your eyes.

We are of the second fall because the knowledge that was granted has been lost due to the burning of books and practitioners during the middle ages. We have become materialistic but seeds of new growth are sprouting. Live to explore and explore to live!

If today people sit in meditation looking at their own ego and call this reflection, how can anything come of it? Beyond the turbulent sea of sense there are signals to follow that will lead to a promised land where divine development occurs for every soul.

A religious practice is never contemptible providing it is the sign of a great and holy thought. Rebuild the alters, purify your temple and hold yourself in readiness for the visit of the Spirit. The sign by itself means nothing. It is the faith you have that sanctifies it. Let the divine rule divinity and let us by God's grace rule ourselves wisely.

When Two Become One

When two become one
The inner person and the outer person
The soul and the mind
The heart and the mind
When they become one
The outer sun and the inner sun
The outer moon and the inner moon
The outer world and the inner world
When the two become one
The one that heals and the one that is healed
The one that gives and the one that takes
The one that is loved and the one that loves
The one that has grown and the one that grows
The one that understands all this and more
That the stars and angels teach us to explore
When the two become one,
The abled and the disabled
The rich in spirit join the spirit that is rich
Rich and poor become wealthy and healthy
The unhappy become happy
The dull becomes interesting

The future becomes the present
And hell becomes heaven

Then the two become one, the soul and the spirit
The heart and soul and the brain and the mind
When the two become one

The male and the female
The beginning and the end,
The maker with the made
The made with the creator,
The well and the unwell
The plant, the tree, the flower, the scents spell

The mountain pebble and crystal cell
The bird , the fish, and all animal power
When the two become one
The being of becoming and the unbecoming of being
The nature of all and all of nature
The laughing and the crying
The spoken and the unspoken
The light and the darkness
The solid and the fluid
When the two become one
The sister and the brother
The mother and the father
The begotten and unbegotten
The natural and the unnatural
When heaven and earth unite ,
Inside and out , left and right
As above and so below,
The alpha and the omega
When the two become one ,
Those that hurt become hurt and learn
That those who forgive are forgiven
Those that love become loved and
Those that know are known
When all become nourished with and
By the enlightened and divine one
Forever our protector and saviour
When the two become one

Chapter Three

PRACTICE MAKES PERFECT

Druid means he who knows. The purpose of Alchemy is not to make something out of nothing but to fertilise and nurture the soul within. Much knowledge has been lost but I will show you how to do this.

When you have found the beginning of the way, the star of your soul will show you the way. That light is the calm spirit that inspires the soul and nurtures it. Find it and follow it.

Opening the doors of the soul is a herculean task, but one we must all do sooner or later. The raising of oneself into an individual power of Astral significance is a goal worth achieving in this life. I believe it is why we are here. Otherwise we are like the hapless hamster on a wheel. Doing what we have always done because we do not known how to break the cycle of mind mould. If there is a problem in our life it can often be as a result of the mess within and the self sustaining confusion we are all prone to on occasions where the truth lies buried in a pile of lies

Self awareness brings self improvement. I work night and day to improve myself. I do it by self exploration and self witnessing. How I respond to others around me and to myself. I stay true to my cherished beliefs without offending others. I help not hinder.

Live neither in the present, past, or future but in the eternal. That is the right place because your mind will be focused on the spiritual and not only on the material or physical world. With your mind focused thus many things will become revealed to you.

If love is the language of the Astral plane then the emotion of love is the tool with which we must work and perfect. Pure selfless love and unconditional compassion, empathy, and good will to all. Recognise ignorance when we see evil and convert it if possible.

All steps are required to make up a ladder to help you reach your destination. When you reach a life beyond individuality then you know you are ready to climb the ladder. The journey of the soul towards God is the ultimate task of life.

When the soul comes to power, meaning it's existence is recognised and nurtured by you, it makes a body in it's own image. The mirror of the imagination reflects the light of our participation. The empire of the world is the empire of light within you.

Only wisdom is free. Disordered passions are the kingdom of folly and folly is fatality. God is the soul of light. Heaven is the harmony of generous sentiments, Hell is the conflict of cowardly instincts. To know all this is to create a positive life.

When we become children at heart we stay young in mind body and spirit. All the triumphs of ambition are not worth a single minute of heroism and charity. To unify both sides of our brain is unicameralism , to unify an argument pure humanitarianism!

Happy are those who find immortality in the creation and nurturing of their soul. Know that your soul is growing inside of you. It lives forever so take care of it. It is conscious and remains so, long after your body dies.

God's love is the light. When you see the light it will change and you will change. Love your soul and do things that please it. Become children at heart and you will remain young. Know that without the light of God humans cannot conceive of what they see.

The 'Great Work' is worthy of enquiry from those who know they have the highest order of mind. The mind is the builder of the person and the soul. Mind exists beyond the limits of space and time and is not limited to the brain. It is an empire with no limit.

When the spiritual self is able to open the seals on the spiritual chakras then the messiah is born within us. Whatever you dream of you can do, so make a start. You don't need to tell me when you see the light. I will know as the light will burn brighter.

We are light , we are spirit. A flower of light watered by the spirit of life. Brain, body, mind, and soul fed by a spirit of light. We are all a little I am in the great I am of Spirit. Salaam, Namaste. May the spirit of the hidden one be with you always.

The day of the harvest draws near. Open the hidden and invisible eyes of time and eternity. Seek the light within at night when it is easier to see so that it will shine in you all day. Light gives thought to form and form to light. Now go create!

Play with the light rays, create your light world. Do not close the seeing eye that returns your gaze or hide away from the light of its beloved countenance. Learn by practising to see with the inner eye. Built the light by paying daily homage to it. Do not be impatient. Failure is a test of you and your patience. We all have to go through it to succeed. Stay free in spirit and believe. Do not allow the light in you to be obscured though you will find it easily is. When or if this happens simply ask and it will return to you.

The young have much to learn, the old have much to learn, so stay young at heart then you will learn much. Judge the teachers by their works, the speakers by their words, the preachers by the outcomes and the poet by what is known of it!

The soul is travelling in the body, a journey of one lifetime on Earth or of many. All depends on the relationship with mind and whether it sees the light or not. Have a clear quiet mind and then you will see the light. We are all time travellers. Namaste.

I have been to the place called the Astral plane. It is a divine dazzling light filled realm where there is no such concept as time and space as we know it. A place where the past is always present as a kind of implicate order on which to build our future dreams.

Some of you have made headway, others are not there yet. Spiritual insights are evidence in themselves and do not need empirical proof. In your meditations shut your physical eyes and open you inner third eye. Trust in yourself and see the light.

The book that must be opened, the book with the seven seals read of in Revelation may refer to the human body. In the spirit of the 'Lamb of God' may we safely open the seals of the spiritual centres within us.

All of us should attempt to perfect ourselves in this life. It is not hard to learn what must be done to achieve improvements. All we have to do is to watch our behaviour and listen to ourselves with regard to those around us. Look for the good in everything.

Our earthly life is scripted by the soul and laid out in a manner that promotes growth and development. But consciously we can play our part by developing a personal code of conduct. May the darkness of the past be transformed into the dazzling light of the future.

To search for selfish reason will lead you away from knowledge. So if you would succeed in the 'Great Work', and we all must sooner or later, seek to help humanity and the world evolution will bring you one step closer.

Every idea that becomes an ideal for you also creates forces of light and life within you. Meditation is a road to super-sensible knowledge. Therefore if you would have more give more so that your day of accomplishment draws nearer. For succeed you will.

Mystics have often told of the divine light that is within us. I am not alone in what I say. *Rudolf Steiner* said; 'Everyone who focuses on the simple processes with persistent rigour and complete patience will be led to a perception of the inner manifestation of light.'

Who we think we are depends on our awareness and perception of what constitutes reality. It stands to reason that those who understand and see more of themselves and what they are truly made of have a more meaningful knowledge of self and their abilities.

Try not to reflect on what you are or who you may become but rather on what you have already been and will always be. Do all you can to get to know your true soul. On the day you enter into full embodied and empowered awareness, you will live and breathe your own spiritual epiphany.

The three stages of the 'Great Work', Preparation, Initiation, and Illumination, do not have to occur sequentially. It is not necessary to complete one stage fully before moving to the next. Let your inner light be your guide.

Do not be disappointed if progress has not manifested in the way you had expected. You may have progressed quite far spiritually even though materially you see no change. Weave backwards and forwards through the various stages of spiritual growth and love life.

Take time to understand the processes and changes that are taking place within you. Do not rush them. Allow the time necessary for the processes to evolve. Learn to listen to the quiet voice within. It will teach and show you many new things.

The higher beings of the spiritual world will speak to us once we have learnt to listen selflessly. Learn to move through pleasure and pain with the same amount of dignity. Will yourself into a complete spiritual and material being. Unite the two if you can.

A golden rule of spiritual power states for every single step that you take in seeking knowledge of hidden truths, you must take three steps in perfecting your character to the good. Learn to build the light in yourself for that is the empire of the world.

No matter a person's spiritual insight or their knowledge of their inner soul, Dreams provide an opportunity to learn about our inner person or soul. Until we are are at one with the being we have always been, the soul must reach out to us in our quiet moments.

Vanity is useless. We must learn to progress without an ulterior motive. The forces at work in the world are those that we see and feel and those we cannot see or feel. Be aware of all that happens to you today and ask why. Then you will learn much.

Without human understanding all steps are in vain. The actions of the initiated are often misunderstood. Be aware but fear not to open your soul to the world of souls, your spirit to the universe of spirit and your mind to all possibilities.

Our bodies, brain, soul and mind must be in perfect harmony. The soul is free to express itself fully poised in perfect balance between the senses and the spirit. As seers we must not become dreamers. Seers are always awake even as they sleep.

To try and perfect oneself is not a selfish but divine act. The soul permeates both the physical and ether body. Learn to regulate the currents that run through both. Learn to breathe in through all your senses the element of light.

Happy are you who awake. Blessed are they who open the eyes of the blind and say from the heart; 'You are the perfect day and in you dwells the divine light.' It is my happiness to know and understand the minds of the past so that our future may be assured.

Seek knowledge so you may learn, so you may be taught! No one can learn well without reading much. I have read much and so I teach. Hidden within everything that you see is something that cannot be seen by ordinary sight. Learn to see with eyes tightly shut.

We were poor humans, sad beings who could not or would not see their own light. We were only half of who we might have been. An Astral being that was forbidden to express itself. We had eyes, ears, speech and power, yet used none of these inner gifts and instead looked to artificial intelligence to provide for our future needs.

Reality will unfold itself to us but we will not see and feel it until we have the correct perspective, heightened awareness and the knowledge of how to experience the Astral plane.

The soul needs the teachings of the inner spirit. In the sacred marriage there are three. The spirit, the soul and the mind. The three must marry to create an Astral being who is a worker of the light. Remember light creates energy and matter.

Light has intelligence and rules of conduct. To work the light one must be at one with the intelligence and know the rules of behaviour.

Loneliness is a state of mind not a state of being. If you are lonely get to know your soul then you will have many friends. Some on this plane of awareness and some on the Astral plane. To know your divine self? Well now wouldn't that be quite something!

The winds of Earth may still themselves, as the winds of heaven may roar. Intelligent breath whispers through our greater mind. But are you listening? To know that God exists for you should be enough to spur you on to great things. Ah imagine those silver wings!

The winds of Earth will still themselves also the winds of heaven.

The intelligence breathes in, into the innermost chambers of our greater mind where non-stop creation occurs, and where everything we can think or hope for happens. Listen to your mind.

How does existence which has no being, appear in a power that has being? Get to know your divine part and empower your soul. Begin by having a relationship with your inner self, build trust, ask questions, listen to the inner voice and learn!

Prayer is like the soul breathing. The difficulty of the task melts in the desire to reach divine contact. If you know the truth, the truth will set you free. Remember this, no matter where you are, it is where the mind is that counts. In the knowledge of this lays your treasure my dear friend.

Divine mind that makes the light to shine, be blessed by the spirit of the divine eye and welcome in the glorious internal sun. Those of you who have seen this have witnessed the light of God, the soul and all that is within to work on. There are divine beings that dwell in bliss.

There is truth, goodness, light and life. Always have your inner eye search for the glorious spiritual sun that is within you. That sun will provide you with the internal energy that inspires the mind to connect with the soul within you. All this is hidden from those who do not know or seek to understand their Astral self.

Be alive to the things of the soul. When you are awake during the day and when you sleep at night. Make the connection, feel the vibrations of soul awareness. Feel what it is to be really you. See the light in your soul, there in the centre of your being.

You are an energising, creative, listening, selfless mind that glorifies its source. Awake! live! kindle the spark and come alive. This is the 'Holy Grail', the true light within you. Become the cup of knowing. Raise the cup and drink. You are not alone.

To you will be revealed all that is hidden from humanity. You are light, life, and grace. Our world will be revealed when our energising, creative, and listening mind awakes and all that is now hidden will start to emerge from within.

We should spend as much time exploring within ourselves as we do exploring the world. For in the final analysis we are the world. Become a knower and a doer. Ask who exactly within you is doing the thinking. Energise and grow your mind so all will be well.

Make no mistake. It is a race against time to reach our full and unique development before artificial intelligence takes over and makes us all robots. We must come to our senses. Brain waves like radio waves are a form of electromagnetic radiation. Listen!

There are many who refer to the inner light as a way of expressing their spirituality. They have not seen or worked with the light that I speak of that is within each soul. The light is real. Whether you are able to see yours is up to you. Try until you do.

When you know, you will know you know! You will feel radiant with the inner light that leads you forward to truth and knowledge about yourself your soul and your eternal divine Mind. Remember your mind lives forever. Be good to it and nurture it.

After you die you may think you are still alive. That is because your mind, the one you live with now and have always lived with, never dies. Think of all the treasure you have, the abilities that in this life you have never used. Awake and see the light!

Unfold your latent powers and senses that are striving to be unfolded. Do this in the spiritual and material realms. Cultivate a spirit of being that is wide awake all the time. Wide awake to the knowledge that comes to you. In you is the universe.

Creating a ritual will help shift your level of consciousness away from everyday material concerns and allow the spiritual you to connect more easily. It will take time for you to get to know your soul. Make a space for your soul to communicate with you.

God will restore memory because that is the religion of mind. That divine mind that is in each and everyone of us loves your soul very much and when the two are connected through spirit, you become a holy and spiritual person.

By the use of mind the psychic state is turned towards the spiritual realms. A fundamental principle of mind is to observe that which is not oneself! Then you will see what secrets are revealed. Only then does your real journey begin. Take the time and communicate constantly with your inner self.

Our unconscious mind is a bridge between the cosmic realm and the spiritual realm of God. When you see the light within it is an assurance of God's presence. We are a little of the great 'I am of Spirit'. Awake to the full potential of your mind. See the light!

Here in the words of this book lies the hope and search for the soul of humanity. Happy is the person who finds themselves and their place within, where the light shines eternal.

Now think of the universe as your home and explore it any time of day or night. Explore the things you cannot see, hear or feel, until you can see, feel, and hear ! Naturally this takes time. However it is certainly your duty to learn all that there is to learn about your life. The seen and unseen. Your mind is a time machine. Go explore. Then give praise and thanks to God for the knowledge you have received

Chapter Four

THE LIGHT KINGDOM

And a voice was heard from heaven, The elect shall possess light, joy and peace and they shall inherit the Earth. And they shall see the light and find righteousness with the Lord of Spirits. *Enoch IXIV.4*

In the first book of Pistis Sophia; Jesus instructs his disciples into the mystery of the 'Light Kingdom.' For I have said to all, they are to seek the mysteries of the Light Kingdom which shall purify them and make them refined and lead them into the light'. 'Cease not to seek day and night and remit not yourselves until ye find the mysteries of the 'Light Kingdom' which will purify you and make you into refined light and lead you into the 'Light Kingdom.'

The Pistis Sophia is a wonderful book and I recommend that you read it. However the aim of my book is to help you find your Astral self and to understand that your soul and mind does not die away even though the physical body and brain do.

Consider seriously what this means for you and your life. Consider how you may feel about this knowledge and how it will affect the decisions you make in your everyday life from now on. Imagine the awareness of who you are continuing after the death process when you find yourself in a new dimension of being. There on what I call the Astral dimension of awareness, you will be with other Astral beings, some you may know and some you may not.

Who are the knower's and possessors of the light and who has the light knowledge? Ask yourself this question and wait for the response. If you are a natural light worker you will know what to do, but I am also here to help you in any way I can. To know is to be able when one dares to will!

I enjoy telling you that you are the perfect day within whom dwells the perfect light. But as a disciple do not blindly follow instead but be wide awake, alert and ready to learn. Be ready to be guided and lose all arrogance. Then the light will appear to you, not in a dream but in all reality. You will be enlightened. Imagine your joy. I recall mine. I was uplifted.

No one can judge what I say without having tested or investigated the relevance and profound nature of my message. Condemnation without investigation is the highest ignorance. Cometh the hour, cometh the message. Raise yourself up and many will follow your example.

Water becomes holy when the divine rays of light shine upon it and it is blessed with love and peace. Drink the light you have been told how! Drink the holy water, you have been shown how! Do it in faith and remembrance and love of the divine in us humans.

When I speak of light I mean actual light! Many speak of light but they do not actually mean the *Divine Light.* They are speaking metaphorically or speaking of something else entirely. When they read the ancient writers who spoke of light they assumed it was a metaphor for knowledge. But I believe that when the wise ancients wrote of light they actually meant the light that resides inside of us.

These same writers are trying to teach you to be a spiritual person. But mark me, I am not trying to teach you to be a spiritual person. You already have a spiritual side to you. I only want to help you know yourself fully. I will help you make a closer and more communicative connection to your soul and divine mind so that you become more than who you are at the moment. It is not me that does the miracle but you.

As a rule we only live in a small part of ourselves. When we awake we find there is so much more to the world and us. The time is coming when we must all awake to our true nature and our true destiny. You are aware that time feels like it is speeding up. That is why I think we should prepare now.

I have said to you that this knowledge has been lost for many generations. Be under no illusion, you are one of the first generations to hear this message again. In that respect you are chosen. But all humans will know this message sooner or later.

Again I repeat, Your body and brain will die but your mind and soul will not. Your personality will continue to mature through many lifetimes, some on this planet others not. Where you go depends on your intention. Believe in the light. Be children of the light.

Within your total manifestation of being exists all the material required to help your soul and personality evolve. Everything that has ever been or will ever be in the conceivable time-frame that we refer to as life. Your body is physical and ethereal, your mind and soul Astral in nature.

Humans possess a subtle body controlled by chakra-like energy centres. Spontaneous last life recall is relatively common in children. As we age we have managed to shut ourselves off from our full perceptual capabilities. This has to be reversed.

We are still children when it comes to understanding the true nature of time. Our understanding of time itself must change. Think about what all this means for you.

It may be that you somehow knew or had a certain feeling that this might be true but were frightened to say it. Well listen to your intuition and pay attention to what else it may be telling you.

It is clear the world is changing. We recognise now that there is far more to us than meets the eye! By that I mean our attitude towards ourselves, who and what we are will change once we recognise that death is not the end for us. We will change on the inside and this will make a difference because we will see the whole world differently.

None of us should be here to change the planet. The planet is perfectly capable of changing itself if it so wishes. It is a holistic being after all.

We are here to grow into our own reality, to know that when we have fully formed we will become an 'Eternal Being' of absolute exquisiteness which will have access to boundless knowledge and enjoy universal ability living on a terrestrial planet called Earth. Time will have a whole new dimension for us as we enter into a cosmic awareness and holistic consciousness with each other.

Ask yourself why it is that we have not yet come to agreement on the common good for all humanity. It is one rule for us and one rule for them. It is a great pity as we do have the answers and we can make life better for everyone. Why are we so afraid to trust each other? Is it because we are so fond of exploring and changing the world physically but not so fond of exploring ourselves internally and spiritually?

How can it be that the planet has lost sixty percent of its wildlife since the 1970's? How can the world and its life forms exist if we do not change? The world is not a better place because we are not better people! But all that can and will change. We have nothing to fear once we truly know ourselves for we shall know ourselves to be of divine origin and then we shall do divine things.

To control the heart chakra is to control one's destiny. 'Take a cup of water with sugar at its bottom. You sip the water and it is tasteless but stir it and it becomes syrup. Likewise the heart, the heart is like a cup and divinity lies at the bottom.' *Sai Baba*

We are truly the makers of our own soul. We are often reborn with those we have known in a past life where some debt and or affection is due for repayment. To progress we must be aware of this.

We are what we are as a result of many experiences lived over many lifetimes. We are all mothers and we are all fathers to the soul within. We all have a responsibility to nurture our baby. If you honour another soul, and many of us do, then at the very least honour and know yours.

To increase the power of your mind you must try to have at least one original thought a day. This will not come easily as normally only geniuses are capable of such things. By original I do not mean of material benefit but spiritual. To be original it must come from your soul and mind. It will not be easy.

It will be like trying to open a locked door. But continue by seeing that locked door open in front of you. Do not worry if you do not succeed straight away. I have said many times that the process cannot be rushed. It is different for every soul.

If at first you don't succeed, try, try, and try again. It is the trying that opens the door.

With your mind learn to see the lamp which shines from the soul. Your inner sun can shine much brighter if you would only acknowledge that it exists. By searching you will find it and once having found it you will be a very happy person indeed.

Concentrate the seed flower of light above the human body in the eyes of the mind. Somewhere in the darkness that you see, when your eyes are closed, is the light that I speak of. Feel the teleportation of soul energy go through your mind as you search. Somewhere between fire and darkness lies the light.

Those who are free of sin can make God’s light flash. Jesus’s light was always with him from the beginning to eternity.

The light flower of the individual passes through heaven and covers earth. All is connected. All is one. Light streams - light and water; life streams- water and light. Once you see your light you can never forget the experience. You are changed because you have become one with the light.

As you are probably aware our lives are guided by hidden forces and events. Yet that spiritual force is in all physical life and what a force it is! So make the connection between the two within your own mind . Why not try it today?

The luminous nature of light can pass through physical bodies. When the light shows itself, God’s light, neither alters or destroys the matter through which it manifests. There is a perfect light in the heart of all people if only more would search for it.

Pictures are as thoughts in the mind, They are seen by men and women but the pure light that reveals them remains veiled. However on the day that you see the light of your own self you will be amazed and you will then understand you are never alone nor have you ever been alone.

The 'Paradise Lost' myth represents the loss of our knowledge and the loss of our light state of being. Awaken the eye of the mind, awaken your spiritual eye. A spiritual shining picture is the Astral embodiment of the state of soul.

Each soul must study itself and learn whether it has the faculty for further divine enquiry and knowledge. Each must find their own way in the spirit world. Your light power extends beyond your physical form. We are saviours or destroyers of ourselves first of all.

Begin to think of yourself as a multi-dimensional being who has many aspects and many bodies. Awaken to the knowledge that as humans we exist simultaneously in a multi- dimensional being. The physical, astral and causal. Remember through us the Gods live!

Thought produces reality. The development of imagination can help alter the course of human evolution. Don't wait to be entertained but rather learn to entertain yourself with outward and inward skills. Remember the mind is free to come and go with the soul.

The light which you will find within will purify the body of matter and make it into a refined light exceedingly purified. Soul brings the light and life. It cannot abandon itself because it is an eternal being. Search for the mystery of the light.

The soul of the light is the light of the soul. If the light is in you then you should learn how to use it, otherwise why have it?

Within you lies a gateway that opens to the spiritual world. Search and you shall see the light and find righteousness with the Lord of Spirits. The universe will ascend, just as every being will to the Light Kingdom and the Treasury of Light.

The light shines in the darkness and the darkness cannot overcome it. It is dazzling and brilliantly divine. There is no mistaking it and when you see it you will know it. Yet only if you search for it honestly will you see that it shines as a beacon within you.

As you watch with your third eye, the star within will get brighter and more intense. It will start to move follow it as it develops into a vision you recognise and love. Allow it to take you on your own special journey. Salaam, Namaste.

Many times I have asked you to search for the light within. Those that have found it are happy and changed forever.

Here is something to be left for all eternity. My words, our words, my understanding, your understanding of knowledge, not something to lay your hands on but somewhere to rest your weary heart my friend.

We who have witnessed so much terrible suffering now wish to bend the time, adjust the clocks and say enough is enough. Our souls are worthy of far more. The future does not stand in our way, only the past! It is the past that we allow to halt our souls progress. Be not afraid of tomorrow.

Embrace all possibilities for growth and turn your back on the limiting forces that hem you in on all sides. You are the key to solving all your problems. You are the key to your future happiness.

It is time to make personal connections between the spirit and material world by learning to operate in both simultaneously. Do not strive for personal powers or believe that others have greater powers. Concern yourself with your soul.

'To find ourselves is to know our source. We reach towards the supreme seeking communion.' *Plotinus.*

Each and everyone of us is learning how to survive and thrive eternally. As long as divinity in all its forms remains frightening to us we will struggle to free ourselves from the chrysalis of matter. Faith is a voyage of discovery upon the river of life.

It is natural for us to do this . We instinctively know there is more to our life than that which we are currently feeling. Waste no time in searching now! Meditate on the intellectual light. From here comes the spirit of creativity.

The soul becomes the light. Pure, buoyant, unburdened, raised to Godhead and knowing it's Godhead. When the soul loves God and draws nearer to God by nature of its own will it gains a certain participation in God.

'You will see him face to face and be in the presence of the living God that is seen face to face. We are one people and if we grow in belief we will be filled with gates of intelligence.' *Gad; Ch,12; 17-19*

Blessed is the eye that has seen all these things. So be wide awake now! Be ready to be guided and the master will appear. Prepare for the materialisation of the spiritual and the spiritualisation of the material.

Be a worker of the light. Be proud to work the light. Be a protector of the light. Learn to live your life through and for the light. Work for God and God will work for you. You have hands of blessing use them well. You have a God mind within you, find it and develop a proper and honest relationship with it. See the light that mind alone can see.

How blind are they that do not see that physical light is nothing but the instrument of thought. Thought of the mind then reveals the light that is spoken of here. Thought creates it for use and for its own purpose.

There is only one pure light, life. Thought becomes light and light becomes thought. You must learn all about the light inside of you. You must go and find it. I can tell you about it but I cannot find it for you. When you find it you must learn to work with the light. You start by feeling the love and peace it sends you and then it is natural of course to return the sentiment.

I will tell you a secret. It took me a very long time to see my light. That is because I wasn't sure what I was actually looking for. No one told me that I would see a midnight sun shining brightly back at me in the darkness of my mind. It took me over a year and with a concerted effort on my behalf that dispelled all fear of failure. I prayed that I would be guided and that I would see. When the light suddenly shone upon me and showed it's absolute radiance there was no doubt in my mind that this was what I had been looking for. I was changed forever in a second. You will be too when it happens to you so have faith and don't worry about the time it may take you.

Mind mediates between soul and spirit. Search and you shall find. You who earnestly and persistently seek shall find the light I speak of. To you who knocks and believes, the door will be opened.

You have heard it said perhaps that seers must not become dreamers but as dreamers we must not become seers either. What does that mean? It means we must try not to have expectations about wanting to see and feel what is not truly there. In other words we must allow images to appear of their own volition and not of our own making. It is always good to have a reality check every now and again.

Jesus is called the 'Son of Righteousness' because he brings light into the world and light into darkness. Therefore the light you see through your third eye, the light I speak of as the midnight sun is also righteous. Yeshua is the light within us that cannot be hidden. The true light that comes from eternity to give light and revelation for all mankind.

It is not where inspiration comes from that is important. It is where it leads. Where it leads will show that the origin is divine.

Now think about who you really are and what it feels like to be you. You will always be you but your world can change.

Consider this today. If you could go back to a previous life what would you want your soul to put right in this life now? The answer you will receive will empower you and tell you a lot about who you really are without the trappings of culture and religion.

Plotinus said that 'Holy things may not be uncovered to a stranger, to any that have not attained the vision to see'. The soul, your soul must look within. Until the seeing comes you will still be craving something that only the vision of the light can give you.

'Hail to you oh reapers! un-close your eyes, Awake! Possess ye the power of light.

Un-close your eyes and look ye at the light. Seek out the Truth in the mind.' *Plotinus*

May your eyes see when they are closed. Watch for the eye looking back at you and then ask to see the light. May your eyes see the rays of the sun's disc and the multiplicity of ideal forms that emanate in front of you. This is true self awareness. You have heard it said that they eyes are the windows of the soul. A window that looks outwards and a window that looks inwards.

We are always looking out. Sooner or later we must also look in. Expect to see a world every bit as interesting and even more colourful that the outside view. The eyes are the windows of the soul and through them the spiritual and physical worlds connect.

Do not forget why this personal light-work is so important for your soul. You do not die! Your mind survives death. How you end up feeling on this earth is quite likely how you will feel when you are dead. Therefore make yourself happy and content by serving others well. Your mind and soul live until the end of eternity. Your outer shell, your brain and body die as your soul and mind passes on.

Depending on your advancement in this life you may be reborn on this planet or in another dimension, or plane of awareness.

If you are reborn you may only remember your previous existence up to the age of about four. After this age memories of the current life become ingrained and the memories of your past life become less active. Remember at any point in our life we could find ourselves surrounded by an Astral light.

So how do we work the light within us? Well the occult 'Light Principal of Vitalisation' means we must learn to give life to the light.

This means controlling our energies through our mind to actively encourage the light to shine in us and on upon us. We have to learn how to work with the light that is within us so that it may shine brightly and divinely.

Recall the auras that surround the heads of saints in paintings, or the Aura of our Lord and of all holy people in the ancient icons of the old masters. This is the light I am speaking of and the one I wish you to develop for yourself.

Plotinus said 'Heavens exiles stray from the orb of light.' We can be forgiven for not knowing. But once we know we should act if we wish to evolve.

So may the light always shine within you. May you receive the blessings of the great light being who is our messiah, our lord and son of God, and our saviour. For the light is with you and within you. You yourself are with the light and you are the light. Receive the mysteries of the light so that you will inherit the light Kingdom. Be bearers of the light. Be righteous and good. Receive the light in the eyes and know the light stream belongs to the Astral plane. Amen

Chapter Five

MIND AND SOUL

'Therefore it seems to me a very foolish man and truly wretched, who will not increase his understanding while he is here in the world and ever wish and long to reach that endless life where all shall be made clear.' *Alfred the Great.*

Is it possible to know where the life force in humans comes from? Since it is so attracted to the physical being it must have a magnetic quality about it. A magnetic light quality radiating and nourished by the interaction of a physical and spiritual body. That magnetic quality diminishes with age and the soul is less harnessed over time. But we can do far more than we currently do to keep that magnetic link between soul and body at its optimum level once we realise that this is within our power and is a choice that we all have.

We are made into being by our own forces of mind. Speech language and grammar all have their effect on who we think we are. Our minds can become a much more varied store of creativity if we do not lock them it into cultural limits but stay as free as a bird.

We naturally want to organise ideas, and objects into things that have meaning or use for us. We do not enjoy disorder yet within much of the disorder is a kind of order or meaning that we do not understand yet could have meaning and be very useful!

Creation should never be a selfish act but something that is done for the greater good. Our minds and our ideas have an inclination to evolve. That is a good thing. If we fixate on what we want all the time we block the process and become a non creator.

Though our reasoning, logic and emotions set the agenda for our daily life, this is not the way of the spirit and soul which is to guide love and grow, and to nurture all beings and help them play their part in existence. That is surely divine work.

All truly great scientists have seen and understood that within the structural processes of the universe both great and small there is a vast harmony that could only be driven by an intelligent mind. This mind I call God and I worship it.

Within the pages of this book lies the battle for the soul of humanity. Within the words of this verse lies the letters for mind activity. The mind goes forth to search the secrets of its new found home and see what happens when you compare the inner landscape with the outer landscape.

A wholehearted interest will give the mind the energy to see what is new and different and then to put it into some other framework and test its significance. Many say they don't have the time but it is time well spent because from this work fortune arises.

Throughout our work the mind is asked to be both student and teacher. The observer and the observed. How is this possible? It is to do with the all seeing nature of mind and we learn by using our third eye to peer into the void of oneness.

Be a new human of a new Earth. One who takes and one who gives. You are an ocean in which all fish swim. You are the air through which all birds fly. You are the earth through which all trees sprout. Be a new human of a new Earth. One who takes and one who gives. I'm thinking of a new Jerusalem of the future. Blessed is the eye that sees all these things. Be wide awake now.

A student of 'Astral Philosophy' should be a sensible person devoted to clear thinking. I think therefore I am. And I am therefore I think!

You may have heard it said that only by joys and sorrows does a person learn about themselves and their destiny. They learn what to do and what not to do. But I say go within deeply and learn to see with eyes shut, to feel with heart open, to hear the angels sing and to create your own paradise within. Then with a happy heart give of yourself to those who need you knowing that all your energy will be repaid by the loving God that resides within you.

All this I say when I say see the light. All this I mean when I say be the light. We are energy beings and God is love and light.

As humans we individualise everything. But soul is not like that. You will know this when the power of the most high overshadows you. You are alive and awake when you are awake on the inside and the outside. Mark me well, you are the author of your life.

The way to real power is to be humble and sacrifice yourself to a greater good. It means giving yourself up to inner and outer progress and to the common good. Soul is a spiritual being whose power must be made manifest through your mind. Listen to it.

Ancient temples are books to those who can read them. Likewise the body. Soul must study itself to learn and bring about the spiritual evolution of the person. Some of this work is done in dreams. Dreams are not always what they seem, so study them well.

'For all the day they view things unrespected
but when I sleep, in dreams they look on thee,
And darkly bright, are bright in dark directed'.
Shakespeare Sonnet 43

The great poet was speaking of the inner light that we must all one night see. Better sooner than later. The light is the calm spirit that inspires the soul. It warms it.

According to the writer *Tertuillius,* Hermotimus soul would depart his body while he was a sleep as if on a trip. Many people to day experience and record what they call an 'Out of Body Experience' and they have written books about their journeys.

Robert Monroe was one of many who wrote extensively on the subject. His books are fascinating and the Monroe Institute that he founded is still continuing with research and promoting his work today. So it is clear that the ancients knew as much as we do about the soul's journey but today we have the science to prove it.

However let us also remember that much progress developing inner spirituality is achieved by faith alone. If you did not have the faith in the first place you would not attempt to discover and explore your inner self.

In our innocence we think that knowledge once discovered stays discovered but much has been lost to us. We are only now beginning to find out the truth about our spirituality and for that we must thank the intrepid mystical explorers who have risked ridicule on the world stage to write about their experiences. While we are at it we must pay homage to those educated women who were burnt as witches for practising and promoting their craft of spirituality and healing.

To often these days people know what they think and frequently speak their thoughts aloud. But often they don't know how to think. Their thoughts are in control of them. Just like their emotions. A mature person is in control of emotions and thoughts and examines their reasoning before taking action.

Open the Astral stargate within your mind. Regenerate! The light is the calm spirit that inspires the soul. It warms it as the soul warms to it.

A healthy mind likes to create just as a healthy body must breath. To awaken the creative state of the mind we only need to recreate what it is we see. Likewise on the Astral plane we require our Astral senses to be working in harmony with our mind.

Cultivate and develop your knowledge of the Astral life. The soul is the link between the outer body and the starry spirit beyond. See the flashing eye of the Lord. The 'Aten', the eye of the mind.

Our minds are far more than just the output of our brains. Our minds receive and send thoughts and they guide us through our life. Our mind has its true home on the subtler levels of reality such as the Astral plane.

Ancient people like the Aborigines understood this when they said that the true source of the mind is in the transcendental reality of Dreamtime.

Many wonder at the saying ‘As above so below’ . What does it really mean? Well I take it to mean that the ancient writers, perhaps even Hermes himself, actually meant, As without so within.

There is an outer sun and there is an inner sun. The outer person sees the outer sun and the inner person sees the inner sun. But we are involved with the materialisation of the spiritual and the spiritualisation of the material. It means that the inner person must be able to see the outer sun and the outer person must be able to see the inner sun as well. Then you are a whole and happy person.

Everything in this world is a distraction to those that are easily distracted. If you find yourself unable to concentrate ask yourself why and ask that you may know something of the real world that is within you. Ask that your soul listens to you. Ask so you may receive the answer. Be patient and humble . Remember a rose always blooms divinely.

When entering the Astral plane have a direct thought or purpose otherwise you may as well go and play in a playground. You will learn some games and lessons just as you do on the material plane. And just as on the material plane, the lessons won’t always be immediately obvious. But be assured your Astral knowledge of who you really are will begin to increase. Do not worry about Astral capabilities just yet. No toddler expects or even wants to break a world athletic record let alone get a gold medal!

Always remember the divine beings give but they also demand that you give before you can be their kin.

From here to eternity make a start on developing the Astral and physical self in unison so they become used to each other and become one.

Mind exists beyond the limitations of space and time. Mind is not limited to the brain. Our subconscious mind is a bridge between our cosmic realm and the spiritual realm of God.

The essence of the pure divine light within you is immortal. Mine sometimes has the fragrance of roses. What flower essence is yours? I write this to teach you how the spirit and sense can be united and the two become one.

If we feel that what we search for is impossible or alien, then we feel the search is futile. But if we develop a relationship with our search, if we love the searching and search with faith well then, the answer is not only possible but clear to us.

Mankind is still a generation without a kingdom. If one is saved then all shall be saved. See the light and awaken from your mortal sleep. Become aware of your immortality. Soul is the author of all living things. Your soul is part of the divine soul of God.

If we are poor in spirit it's because of our ignorance of the light we have within. That light can teach us so much and is connected to the Divine. It is a smartphone that we carry with us always and everywhere but sadly some never bother to switch it on.

Our soul is neither male nor female but Androgyne. The Androgynes sin caused them to lose their second sight leaving them only corporal vision. But we can regain it. Know yourself honestly through prayer and meditation and see the light again.

The visions I speak of will be seen through your mind guided by your soul who always knows what is good for you. There the beings of the primordial light will be seen. It's a place where we come from and it is where we go after the body on earth dies.

A seed is useless unless it is planted in fertile soil. For where the mind is so is the treasure but you must first seek the kingdom of God. Every seed is part of the kingdom of God. Astral powers most definitely bring about material change. Respect them.

No scientific or mechanical tube has yet discovered the nobler and more gifted things that hover in the illumined air, other than the human mind and soul. The eyes of truth are always watching over us. For where the mind is so is the treasure.

Our natural inclination is to search for knowledge deep within and our natural religion is within us too. Life itself has speech and is always teaching us something. There is a harmony to our life, a rhythm that makes us feel happy. It is not hard to find.

A pronouncement from the 'Temple of Wisdom' said; 'A soul cannot develop and progress without an appropriate body because it is the physical body that furnishes the material for its development.'

Our soul is clothed in a physical body while here but what type of protection will it require for other realms that it will pass through after it passes over at death? It will require a vestiture of love and compassion that it has shown through it's life.

We are all born with differing skills and talents and our job is to explore them in our life. To leave the planet more developed as a soul, as an entity. We are all born with different spoons in our mouth and each of us has an individual path to follow. Who is to say which is good and which is bad? Which is unfair or fair? Who is to say where and how we will end up along our chosen path? So we might as well be conscious of what is actually happening to us and try to understand the process. That way we grow as we go!

Creative energy is our guiding light, all knowledge, science,music, art, and poetry, created by the individual (the few) is created in their mind for the many.

Where is the new light of our time to come from if not from the creative wellspring of the individuals mind open to the cosmic powers of regeneration? How can an individual be motivated to receive the knowledge if not by an inner belief that the power does in fact come from somewhere? In this respect faith is the mother of creation. The pendulum has swung to the right, then to the left. Now it's in the middle. So where do we go from here?

The Beauty

All harmony, all marvel, she,
Above the world and passionless
She rests serene shame fastedly
In her triumphant loveliness
She looks around her, left and right
She has no rival and no peer
The beauties of our pallid sphere
Have vanished in her blinding light
Bound for whatever be your goal
Though to a lover tryst you speed
However precious in your soul
A day dream, you may hide and feed
Yet, meeting her, unwillingly
You of a sudden dazed and mute
Shall halt devoutly to salute
Her beauty and her sanctity.

Alexander Pushkin

We all serve humanity by identifying with the whole world. Be ready to make unselfish sacrifice for it at any moment by living well. Your life is not your own to do with it what you will but rather, it belongs to the forces that work within you.

Why travel the world when there is a whole universe left unexplored inside of you? You are a time traveller, no shame in that! Every inventor and explorer fastens their interest on the unseen. Go build you brain to absorb the finer sentiments of mind.

Through all times, the signs and tokens of that which is beyond matter have been ignored by those of matter.

The time is at hand when science will realise that spirit is always coming and going materialising and dematerialising through us, within and without.

All through time the immaterial has been overpowering the material. It is like that with our thoughts and prayers. Spirit is the great life power on which all matter rests. The labourer is worthy of hire. Ask and you shall receive.

Our thought will produce and shape our reality and because we see our reality through the perception of our thoughts the two are closely intertwined. That is why it is important to always think of the consequences of your thoughts not only upon your reality but also upon the reality of other people.

Also thought is like a wave that moves in and out of your body and brain and surrounds your soul too. You literally cloth yourself in your thoughts. If you want harmony, and who doesn't, then be harmonious and do not fear the future but love the present.

Be free. Do not blind yourself with prejudice that limits your growth or fasten yourself to the treadmill of popular thought or slow the turning wheel of your soul in any deep rut of life. Be aware of the material limitations that you put yourself through.

Greatness of soul is attained by growth. It is not something you are necessarily born with. It is something you yourself build. Development continues for as long as you are here and for as long as you wish it. Our mind is capable of everything.

Emotions can be driven by animal instincts or by divine intelligence. Our entire species became aware at once and now oscillates between the two. True alignment of the mind soul and spirit brings many benefits. Care for all and do not be a sleeping God.

One cannot hurt another human being without hurting oneself. One cannot hurt an animal without hurting oneself.

You are not responsible for your ancestors actions only for your own. God knows what you have done in the past and what you need to do now.

Now mark me. You are a powerful spiritual being that creates your own reality. There is life after death. Your mind does not die! Therefore let us awaken to a new vision of what lies beyond death and what it means to really be alive.

The key to human evolution is our ability to consciously experience our own spiritual essence. Think about what this actually means and what you have to do to succeed. Become a courageous explorer of your consciousness.

Some cannot see the light at first. But if you keep searching as I have taught you, eyes closed, and third eye open you will see it. How you ask? It is simple. In trying to see the light you actually clear the route that has been overgrown by lack of use.

Reawaken your spiritual powers that lie asleep dormant in you. There is a third state of consciousness and it is where you work the light. Be not only a keeper of the light but a nurturer of the light too! Once you are awake you will be awake eternally.

Solomon, Sol, Om, On, the name of the sun and supreme light in three different languages. It is the spirit of universal illumination of the mind, body, and soul. Illumination means lighting up the darkness and seeing as never before. Awake to your true self.

The Christ spirit is within your soul. Use your inner eye to find it and allow it to appear. Welcome the vision and divine aura of the Christ walking towards you with open arms. Nothing is covered that shall not be revealed nor hid that shall not be seen.

The higher states of consciousness and awareness refine the lower states so that they absorb the finer sentiments of a holy mind. What is required? Well more curiosity and bravery since it is right to honour and acknowledge the higher beings in your life.

We must keep improving our God given design by recognising that there is much more to us than can be seen. Personal progress depends on our spiritual intention and our spiritual intention depends on our personal progress!

We have reached the peak of our physical development. Any further improvements are likely to be artificial. Now is the time to reach the pinnacle of our spiritual development. Metamorphosis, the act of changing while still alive is possible. Try!

Retrospection is essential for the development of a spiritual mind.

'A boy I was then did a maid become, a bird, a plant, and in the vast sea swum.' *Empedocles*

Union with the soul constitutes immortality. Wake up now to your new reality.

Divine Well-being

Rare indeed are the calm souls who reach so high
By uniting their hearts with God they learn to fly
Alas some still put all their faith in conquest
And for this reason they claim no rest
Rare indeed the souls that glory in nirvana
Those who do, understand all about karma
Able to enjoy the present moment of infinity
Determined to get the most from their divinity
Rare indeed to know the truth absolute
And your heart to find a steady root
Even though all sorrow and grief
Is the cause of such familiar belief
That delusion and fear, makes us slow

Is caused by our reluctance to let go
All that we can see though it may deceive
Yet far more precious is that which we perceive

A sacred mantra we may wish to conceive
The names of God are many or so I believe
Shame then that religion has its wars
As if it alone owed allegiance to the cause
With the borrowed light of consciousness
The mind and intellect are stirred from lifelessness
Herald the self, the universe, dwelling in the hearts of all
That God, part of the universe existed before the fall
Alas how few even try to know
The good for them only heaven may show
But instead on earth they seek to be
Ever so flattered and honoured in memory
Mind has but three states of awareness
Dreaming sleeping and wakefulness
I am the last witness to speak these words
Remaining aloof from all the worlds
I am transcendental consciousness
Watch how I transcend all your senses,
Let me transmit an old age secret
Even though humans can't conceive of it!
The greatest calamity to befall mankind
Is not their inability to comprehend the divine self or find
The smallest spark of something so preciously fine
That once thought they become God and divine

You know certain virtues there are
That should have been cultivated by humanity thus far
Truthfulness, kindness, forgiveness and discrimination
Beauty of the mind and its senses, mastery over machinations
Non- injury to any, charity, frankness and contentment
Desisting from idle conversations your amendment
Always seeking the highest truth and serving all beings
Devotion to God who is contained in all their feelings
Birth is a door through which we must travel
And to reach that higher state we must learn to unravel
A human birth is an opportunity indeed

Only from this state can we aspire to be freed
Give up the notion of what may be due to us
Because true happiness comes from the universe
That divine spark made us out of an image of love
Given so that we may create freedom just like above
Clinging to wealth and the worldly life
Searching for meaning, trying to avoid strife
Viewed from the outside the root of all misery
Loved from within gives us so much tranquillity
So the bee goes through nature to gather honey
We steal it because we are hungry or to make money
But the blessed bee does not complain
Eager to please it just starts over again

One who has contentment ruling their heart
Feels good and is able to play their part
Discriminating between the real and the unreal
All love conquers hate that's the way they feel
As the restless waves of the mind subside
There arises divine bliss inside
The soul of all souls in all beings
The glory of the divine self is all seeing!
It was not the apple that was to blame
It was not that error that brought us shame
I'm keeping good company tonight
Spending my time with the souls of light
There is a boundless ocean of bliss
Moulded into various shapes like this
Omnipotent, infinite, absolute, impersonal
It's in the heart of all beings and it's incredible
Beyond all name and form and yet
In the souls of all beings I suspect
Words cannot express the glory
Nor the intellect behind the greatest story
Senses may search for inspiration
But their journey ends without confirmation
The mind desperate for conception
Travels a lonely path full of deception

Objects seen, not through the sense of light
Lead on to a heavenly place full of delight
Music heard, yet no harmonic tunes play
The true seer searches at least once a day
Nature revealed in the deepest contemplation
I challenge you to hear my condemnation
To save by playing an honest and brave part
Else from this place in haste you depart!
When the mind becomes divinely absorbed
It sours beyond all consciousness grounded
Then locates the fountain of all knowledge
When you find it remember to pay homage
There is a stream that flows in opposite directions
Like sand in the river, such sparkling reflections
Every soul without distinction is carried by the flow
From wherever they came still they will surely go
There is a bird with colours truly sublime
It twitters a beautiful song in perfect rhyme
All day long and all night it chirps cheerfully
But unfortunately not many are listening!
Only those who have conquered their minds truly
Can hope to conquer the universe fully
Knowing the difference between the real and unreal
They are keen to play by different rules with zeal

In the hearts of all mountain dwellers
There is the artist painting pictures
The musicians playing their tunes
And the poets composing verses
Humanity alone is able to know the highest truth
And attain perfection which is the real wealth
Alas how many think it worthless to try and explore
Or understand God in themselves and even more
Everything in life is so obviously transitory
Still they concentrate on science and the family
I'm not saying that's a bad thing you understand
Just so long as they also explore their spiritual land
Wealth, health, friends, all and more,
A vanishing landscape is not easy to draw
All sorrow and grief are caused by attachment

So learn how to manage freedom enfranchisement
The humans greatest calamitous fall
Is not to comprehend the divine self at all!
Doest thou not understand what is said in this line
Constantly thinking of God makes one divine.
Like a sponge you must squeeze yourself further
To absorb first then make room for divine nature
Understand the universe exists in your place
As surely you do exist in outer space

There are but three states of consciousness
Waking, sleeping and dreaming
And as the witness of I say in truth
Step inside yourself but for heaven's sake stay aloof
For I am calling for more transcendental meditation
A daily routine not something to be done on vocation
Escape the human mind intellect and ego machinations
I am the God of Love and these are not hallucinations
Humans alone are able to know
The highest truth if they can but follow
Then achieve sublime perfection absolute
The only reason why on earth we were put
An uncontrolled mind is our greatest fear
Like driving a car without a gear
Divinely love or else shun
All that was created and all that was begun

Chapter Six

THE LIGHT WITHIN YOU

The light of the body is the eye. If therefore your eye be single your whole body shall be full of light. *Matthew 6:22*

Images are revealed to man but the light within them remains hidden just as the light within themselves is not known. When you know that there is a divine light that is shared by all living creatures then you will cast a beam from out of your eye and truly see.

You are the perfect day. In you dwells the perfect light and in the deepest darkness the light shines even brighter. Remember you are the perfect day with an internal sun that never sets. Learn to shine and spread your rays.

Why do I speak of the light within? It is because reality as we know it unfolds in a non physical way before manifesting on the physical plane. It is the same with us and our hopes for the future. We must learn to understand the hidden nature of ourselves.

The right way is the way of light and all of us must find a way to build the light within us. Heaven is everywhere and in all things. We have to build the light in our Astral being so that it shines brightly and does away with the darkness within our souls that has gathered there during a period of many lifetimes and often not because of any fault of our own.

To do this light building we must turn our personal will into a love of light and of God. When we make room for the Light of God in our soul our life begins to change in ways we would never have expected. The main conclusion to the work is a feeling of peace, enrichment and happiness since you will know that you are and will never be alone.

To enter spiritual reality we have to go deep within our mind. By meditating correctly and venturing into our soul we arrive at an inner world which is at first dark and hazy.

It is here that you must search for the light that I speak of. So close your eyes and open your third eye and immediately see the darkness and feel the energies emanating from that place. Now as if you were literally painting the scene with your eyelashes start to spread the holy light in your mind's eye. Watch as the white brilliant light starts to replace the darkness.

At this time you may start to see colours perhaps even neon lights.

On other occasions you may see the darkness getting less dense and openings appearing. Scenes of relevance to you and your life may appear .

Some will be static others moving. Watch in amazement as a story unfolds. Whatever your experience is, do remember that it is right for you. You are master of your destiny. You always have been and you always will be. All is good.

Each of us has an ancient soul within waiting to be known. Your soul may speak to you in your dreams. Are you listening? Be no longer the person of yesterday but become focused on the soul within you. The soul you have always been but with a few improvements.

To experience the living Christ in your soul means that you are enlightened. It means you must work hard to become perfect. Free the chained up soul. One day we will all know that we don't need to be in the physical body to think, act, or exist.

Sometimes the scenery along the way can divert our attention. We should try not to be diverted from our chosen path and true destination. Mind and mind's eye and the light, They are everything to me. Slowly but surely the Astral dimension dawns in the human mind.

Learning to stimulate your mind to find out all that can be known by intellectual energy brings one closer to God, but when a person is ignorant that they are ignorant what hope is there?

When the mind's eye connects with the universal mind then the divine light shines and brings events from which we learn. Open the shut palaces of the mind and discover all that awaits you because all the pleasures of the earth are not worth one day of holy wisdom.

To expand our perceptive abilities we must find a way of increasing our connection to the Astral plane. Astral plain connections will increase when your mind recognises coincidences that will appear in your life daily. Watch, smile and know.

It is up to each and everyone of us to learn how to travel inwards and upwards along the spiritual path and towards our spiritual essence.

Not only is there power within us but also around us. It is not until we start to develop extra sensory perception that we realise there is much more to us that we at first see. We have been given powerful tools and we can use them by elevated consciousness.

The eye of mind, the true spiritual sun, whose blessed eyes are the countless suns in space, may they shine on you for the rest of your days so that you become a blessed one, a true being of reason and love my dear friend.

When alive in the physical world make sure you love and experience unconditional love. The more love you can give, the more you will achieve, for when you die all this love goes with you in your Aura. May the light of God bring you peace and happiness.

Spirit is the great energy on which matter rests. When the mind asks about a chosen subject with sufficient concentration and good will the answer will usually reveal itself in the actions of those around you or within your own mind. Be observant.

Whilst you have the light believe in the light that you may become children of the light. This means the light will guide and teach you if you allow it. Respect the sacred union between all the different parts of you and allow the connections to take place.

At the heart of all true spiritual experience is the essential interdimensional shift of awareness. By the use of our focused thoughts we mould the energies around us. We are immortal, creative, powerful, spiritual beings. We must learn about our inner self.

Seek the light within so that the power of the stars, the Astral power may grow. The light, having established itself within you will purify and empower your whole being. You become a bearer of the light. An Astral being. So eliminate the chaos and fill yourself with eternal light and love.

The very act of attempting to see the light during meditation or before you sleep or just after you awake will help to activate your third eye and may help in decalcifying your pineal gland so that it functions efficiently.

You should know that you may need to make many attempts but like learning to walk, your success will be assured given the right time for you. You may also notice that you have some changes to your body too. What these changes will be is determined by who you are within. I cannot say that they will definitely happen, only that they may. If there are changes they are changes that are meant to be.

Once you have seen your light, continue to see it everyday if you can. Sometimes you will not be able to see it, or it may seem more difficult but persevere. Patience has its own reward. The time will come when you will see it at will, day or night. You will become aware of it within you as you go through your daily routine. With eyes open and eyes shut. Soon you will see many lights. What follows next will be the natural development of your individual Astral awareness.

Now seeing the light is imperative for your development however, your behaviour is also an ingredient for the fulfilment of the manifestation of light within you. Remember light attracts light! So trust in the light so that once you have seen it, it is always with you even if you struggle to see it. Keep trying until you succeed.

To everyone that sees the light, it will provide the nourishment that you require. That light is pure and powerful. It is love too. The light, your light will give power to those that have faith in it. Allow it to form as a wreath or crown around your head. Sometimes you may experience a tightening sensation as the light tries to connect with you. The 'Elixir of Life' is produced within oneself by learning to rotate the light within.

I am not the first to speak of the light. I will not be the last either. Jesus spoke of the light in Book Two of Pistis Sophia. He spoke about the light and the 'Treasury of Light'.

'Because thou in the mind hast given us mind of the light and hast given us sense and an exceedingly exalted thought.' *Pistis Sophia Ch;83 p;182*

'Do not miss the way that leads from conscious action to unconscious non- action.' Says Master *Lu Tsu,* the writer of the ancient book; 'The Secret of the Golden Flower'. I recommend you read it since it has much valuable information. At its heart, The Secret of the Golden Flower is about 'A secret charm which although it works very accurately, is yet so fluid that it needs extreme intelligence and clarity and the most complete absorption and tranquillity. The magic of the 'Elixir of Life' (I say seeing the light) makes use of conscious action in order that unconscious non action may be attained.

Conscious action consists in setting the light in circulation by reflection (thought) in order to make manifest the release of heaven. If then the true seed is born and the right method applied in order to melt and mix it and in that way create the 'Elixir of Life', then one goes through the pass. The embryo which must be developed by the work of warming, nourishing, bathing, and washing is formed. That passes over into the realm of unconscious non-action. A whole year of this fire period is needed before the embryo is born, sheds the shells and passes out of the ordinary world into the holy world.'

What does all this mean? It means that you cannot rush the process nor should you want to. Like a plant you will take time to grow. The uniting of internal and external methods will be necessary as will acknowledgement of the external and internal seasons of our Astral universe.

There is a time for growth and a time for rest. We must always be aware of and work with the universal energy that surrounds us. It is the inner light that I write of here which is sometimes referred to as the midnight sun because it shines in the dark and in the centre of your being. All changes of a spiritual consciousness depend upon the heart. You cannot wish or pretend to be good, you must be good!

I may say that the light can materialize in a vision of exceptional divinity and beauty. I have seen that happen. When it does the life energy of that vision will gradually permeate your whole being so that you will be filled with the light. The circulation of the light within will quite naturally reduce the darkness. It is the spirit gaining mastery over the body. It is the unification of all. Your soul and mind, your body and brain. By circulating the light one becomes one with the creative powers. This is a message that has not been given for thousands of years.

The soul transmits information to the brain and body by various methods, including dreams, thoughts, visions, inspirations and out of body experiences. At the moment our inner self is neither understood or fully expressed in our culture. But the time will come.

We are evolving into fully conscious multi-dimensional beings capable of inter dimensional travel, awareness and knowledge. A shift of consciousness is at the heart of our out-of-body explorations. We are not always aware that we have travelled.

Total being is to be awake even in our deepest sleep. To remember our dreams and understand why we dreamt them. To allow the higher state of consciousness to refine the lower state of awareness. The awakened mind will help us build a new brain to operate through.

There is a part of us that has never slept, will never sleep and is always awake. While asleep ensure that the work is always productive so that when you awake you feel you have been nourished and can nourish those around you.

When we consider that which is outside of us is also inside of us, and that which is within us, is also outside of us, well then we can only marvel at the miracle called life.

Thoughts are everything. If you would truly know yourself, meditate, forgive and do not be angry.

Better to expand the powers of our mind now than to be ever set in a narrow minded reality. A proactive approach to death is far more sensible than the current cultural dominance of fear loss and despair. Be a courageous explorer of your consciousness now.

To often people confuse the mind with the brain and use the terms alternatively as though they mean the same thing. They do not. They are completely separate . The brain like the body will age and eventually cease to exist. The mind on the other hand lives for eternity as does the soul. It means your consciousness continues after death.

Reality is a construct of your consciousness. Consciousness can be described as the living embodiment and awareness of your mind and soul to a brain and body relationship. Sometimes or too many times it gets stuck into a cycle of actions and decisions of a repetitive nature. If you think back over your life you may be able to see this for yourself.

To develop a closer working relationship with our minds and progress there are many things we can do. We can employ the power of soul and spirit to help us unlock the fixed patterns of behaviour and thinking so that we humans may evolve into an advanced being but first, we have to wake up to the possibilities of a new reality. All will follow after that.

It is quite likely that there are dynamic or very active linkages between mental images that we have of ourselves, and others, and fields of realistic experiences that we all share. Imagery, visualisation, faith and prayer can all heal the body. Constant prayer and meditation will cause both positive and negative images to be impressed upon the energy fields surrounding the body.

Our thoughts can cause holographic images to appear in our aura. You will recall that some religious icons show such images of angels in the aura of the Virgin Mary and Christ child.

It is the constant repetition of such patterns of thought that ingrain themselves so that eventually those thoughts and feelings finally give form or materialize in the body. It may be that by constantly thinking about an illness or imagining what it would be like would be tantamount to giving yourself it and making yourself very ill. Success comes from recognising the threat and doing something about it.

Thoughts should treat the energy field as well as the body. Until many treatments will not be permanent because we have not altered the basic hologram at the mind and spiritual levels.' *Gerber*

Thoughts can also cause images to appear in the subtle energy levels of reality itself. This may explain how the human mind is able to effect miracles and how images from the innermost depths of our minds can take form in actuality such as the physical manifestation of stigmata or other marks on the body, or the reported abilities of *Sai Baba* to manifest at will those items that he gave as gifts to his disciples.

We are literally what we think. Each of us is a universe in miniature as well as being part of the greater universe. We are affected and we effect all that is within and around us.

Death is the transition of consciousness from one dimension to another, from one realm of being to another. No soul dies.

Time and space are fleeting perceptions based only in matter. Soul and mind exist within the concept of time space and matter and outside of it. You can start to experience inner dimensional travel and the Astral dimension now. Eventually we all become spiritual explorers.

'Unless you find paradise at your own centre, there is not the smallest chance that you may enter.' *Angelus Silesius*

A love controlled by time is no love at all.

My soul has slept in many regions as a guest but when I'm home I'm always awake and busy. Well as they say you have to make your own kind of music even if no one sings along! We should become conscious of our Astral being before the end of physical time.

If we continue to think the way we have always thought we will continue to get what we have always got. We will not make fresh headway or see the world any differently. We will simply be moving in circles by making the situation in and around us worse.

There exists an overwhelming sense of pure love. A pure ecstatic state of being that surpasses all form and thought. Some call it Nirvana. In the higher world love is the only motivation for action. So too should it be here.

Follow where destiny leads hand on heart and mind with God.

'A little philosophy inclineth man's mind to atheism but depth in philosophy bringeth men's minds about to religion.' *Sir Francis Bacon*

Your mind is a time machine that stretches back millions of years. The mind can create any reality it wants, meaning that everything is possible. Mind wants to be happy and express itself and it wants you to listen. We can communicate with it if we think holistically rather than in a dualistic manner, which by the way, we often do.

To govern the self is to be able to govern the world. It is about recognising and seeing the greater good and understanding that the personal goal is irrelevant in the wider scheme of things. To serve the greater good is to deny the ego and embrace the all.

The pineal gland and the third eye are part of the operational centre through which the material and spiritual worlds connect. It is never too late to start but first you must awake to the possibility that not only is this is doable, but it is right to do.

We often speak of the physical and spiritual worlds as being separate from each other and separate from us. They are not separate at all. The sooner we understand this the better. It is not wrong to explore who you are and who you might become.

The Light Within

Look again through your mind's eye
With your eyes closed look up at the sky
Where you will see the sun bright and correct
There the radiance when you connect
To that sun with your own soul
If you just have faith in the goal
And if you fail know others have too
But keep trying until you do
Then you will see how much higher
A longing that will quench your fire
Because a love controlled by time
Is no love at all compared to divinity
An eternal love that shines for eternity
When you can so easily reach above
To a divine image of a glorious love
To give all you desire why would you not see
That to follow this advice will set you free
Connect your soul to the inner lights
Your personal show unfolds before your eyes
Now you see the evidence of its brilliance
The glorious evidence of its radiance
A holy divine light that sets you free
Making you into who you want to be

Mind and soul find expression through matter on the physical plane. But both existed long before matter and the physical plane. That is why long after our material bodies cease to exist our mind and soul continue to live and explore the Astral plane.

Chapter Seven

YOUR ASTRAL SELF

Whoever seeks for eternal life must search for the place where from human nature and life originally sprang.

The aim is to develop all the Astral abilities one has been granted and manifest those abilities here on earth as the master Jesus has shown us. Remember he taught us that this is possible and so we are doing the will of God by believing and attempting to develop these skills. In this respect there is no conflict between religious and spiritual belief systems, both past and present.

The improved brain connection with mind and soul must naturally build a new body to physically manifest divine work. This takes time. One example I may give you would be some changes that may occur within your ear structure as you naturally start to tune into higher and lower frequencies.

Through your meditation the undivided effort of spiritual concentration will produce spiritual energy that can create a spiritual existence for you.

Master Lu-Tsu, (796 -880 C.E.) was author of 'The Secret of the Golden Flower.' He wrote extensively about the light. ' When the light is made to move in a circle all the energies of heaven and earth, and of the light and the dark are crystallised. This is seed like thinking, purification of energy and idea. When one begins to apply this magic it is as if in the middle of being there was non-being.'

True spirituality does not only come from what religions teach but from the spiritual universe that is inside of you. From soul state to soul state we attach ourselves to the truths we hold most dear which are the limitless eternal forces of creation and love.

Despite our education and evolution there is still profound disagreement over the most basic issues that affect humanity and life on this planet. Spiritual evolution is gathering speed, therefore we should confront our nightmares and turn them into dreams.

Spiritual action is a thought process of productivity. Our inner reality is played out in pictures, patterns, tastes, smells, sounds, and feelings, added to actions such as running, flying and jumping. To learn we must not only view but ask and question.

Only when the foundation is built can the dwelling be erected.

Open the stargate within your mind to regenerate.

The labourer is worthy of his hire. Ask and you shall receive.

In Pistis Sophia; Ch135; p357; Mary says 'Lo my Lord we have openly, exactly and clearly known that thou hast brought the keys of the mysteries of the 'Light Kingdom' which forgives souls and purifies them and makes them into refined light and leads them into the light.'

The light within has many gifts for you when you learn to work with it.

You must know that when I speak of the light, I really do mean light. In many holy and spiritual writings the term is used in a way that is supposed to mean knowledge or awareness to something new. Whilst both are also true, I only mean light when I say light! When I say to you you will see the light. It is the divine light, a radiating sun that you will see.

While you can learn some things from people, the important knowledge lies tucked away in your soul and mind. The goal of the 'Great Work', or 'Magnum Opus' is to unlock your knowledge that is pertinent to your personal evolutionary growth.

This is what The Secret of the Golden Flower has to say about the Great Work.

'When in the course of time the work is completed and beyond the body, there is a body of non-being (Etheric or Astral body), it is as if in the middle of non being there is a being. Only after concentration work of 100 days will the light be genuine. Then only will it become Spirit Fire. After 100 days there develops by itself in the midst of the light a point of true light pole. Then suddenly develops the seed pearl. It is as if a man and woman embraced and a conception took place. Then one must be quite still and wait.

The circulation of light is the epoch of fire. In the midst of the transformation the radiance of the light is the determining thing. In the physical world it is the sun, in man the eye. The radiation and the dissipation of spiritual consciousness is chiefly brought about by this energy when it is directed outward. Therefore the way of the Golden Flower on the backward flowing method, on meditating correctly, look at the tip of the nose, eyes half open and allow the streams of light to flood in. When one fixes the thought on the midpoint between the eyes, the light floods in. Feel the tightening. (Perhaps tightening in the head or crown) If thoughts occur one can contemplate as to where they came from and where they might lead. Then one should come back to the fixation on the spot between the eyes and make the breathing rhythmical.

The protection of the centre is important for the circulation of the light. Make the breathing rhythmical. Fixating contemplation is indispensable. It ensures the making fast of the enlightenment. It means the circulation of the light.

The human body is a very valuable possession when the primal spirit is master. But when it is used by the conscious spirit, the latter brings it about that day and night the primal spirit is scattered and wasted.' (Meaning perhaps, the energy created is used by the ego or self for material or emotional gain rather than being used for spiritual purposes that fulfil universal requirements.)

Therefore to stay young maintain a passive, peaceful, and positive attitude and love life no matter what it throws at you. The method above allows for the conscious spirit to be subjected and the primal spirit protected so that it remains in control. Mind over Matter.

If the thoughts are held only to the two eyes but the spirit is not crystallized in the solar plexus, the centre in the midst of conditions, it is as if one had mounted to the hall but had not yet entered the inner chamber. Then the spirit fire will not develop, the energy remains cold and the true fruit will hardly manifest itself. Only after 100 days will there develop spontaneously in the light, a point of genuine creative light. Fix your thought on the space of energy, the light of the ear! This is why I have said to you be patient and do not give up. You are to ensure that consciousness is no longer preoccupied with compulsive intentions but turns itself in towards contemplative visions. Detachment of the consciousness from any personal object of desire is paramount.'

In case you get confused here I must confirm that the practice of meditating as suggested above has nothing to do with the method I'm teaching of seeing the internal light that I am speaking of throughout this book. This practice is simply a way of focusing the mind to become free of material everyday thought. It is a good practice to have but do not mix it with the practice of building the light within your mind where your eyes must be closed but your inner or third eye open as you search for the divine light that I have spoken of.

Now here comes a very interesting passage, once again from the Daoist book; The Secret of the Golden Flower; 'The decision must be carried out with a collected heart. The circulation of the light must be united with the rhythmic breathing. For this light of the ear is above all necessary. There is a light in the ear and a light of the ear. The light of the eye is the united light of the sun and the moon outside. The light of the ear is the united seed of the sun and the moon within. The seed is the light in crystallized form. Both have the same origin and are different in name. Therefore understanding (ear) and clarity (eye) are one and the same effective light. One should not be able to hear with the ear the intake or out-take of breath. If the heart is light the breathing is light. Maintain the concentrated breath energy using the crystallized structures in the ear to subdue conscious egotistical energy. When the heart becomes undivided and gathered into one, then the primal spirit wakes to life. The correct way is middle distance between being and non being. Attain purposefulness through purposelessness. Now one can let oneself go through the right way of being, detached and without confusion in an independent way'.

Confirmation experiences during the circulation of light.

'The brilliancy of the light gradually crystallizes, hence a great terrace arises and upon it, in the course of time the Buddha appears. (*I saw Christ walking towards me with arms open*) When the gold being appears who should it be but the Buddha? For the Buddha is the holy Golden Man of the Great Enlightenment. This is a great confirmatory experience. Now there are three confirmatory experiences which can be tested.'

1. Men (voices) are heard talking in the distance, the sounds are all like an echo (or in my case, chanting or bells ring as if from a distant place).
2. As soon as one is quiet the light of the eyes begin to blaze up so that everything before one becomes quite bright as if one were in a cloud.
3. One's body becomes shining like silk or jade. It seems difficult to remain sitting, one feels one is being drawn upwards, this is called the spirit returns and touches heaven. In time one can experience it in such a way that one really floats upwards. (0ut-of-body experience)

So the ancient teacher is speaking of the light attained through meditation that has its roots placed in the energy centres of the body such as the Solar Plexus. It is a light that has been brought in through half closed eyes and is drawn into the body by will power where it is then redirected upwards internally through rhythmic breathing to the eye and ear. Let us be clear here. Master Lu Tsu is teaching very good meditations and quite possibly training the student to manoeuvre what is commonly known as the Kundalini energy up through the body as one does in Yoga. The student is drawing in the light from an external source and then redirecting it up through the body. Whereas I'm saying to you to find the light that already exists in your mind by closing your eyes and opening your third eye. Then see the light. I am not telling you to bring the light in from outside of your body. The light I speak of is a divine light that is already in your mind. You only have to learn how to see it and work with it.

The Embryo of the Tao (From the Secrets of the Golden Flower)

'According to the law but without exertion, one must diligently fill oneself with the light. Forgetting appearance look within and help the true spiritual power. The embryo is the spiritual breath energy of the ego. First the spirit must penetrate the breath energy then the breath energy envelopes the spirit. When the spirit and the breath energy are firmly united and the thoughts are quiet and immobile, this is described as the embryo. The breath energy must crystallise, only then will the spirit become effective. Take material care of the awakening and the answering. The two energies nourish and strengthen one another. Therefore it is said that daily growth takes place. When the energy is strong enough and the embryo is round and complete it comes out the top of the head. This is what is called the completed appearance which comes forth as embryo and begets itself as the son of Buddha. Outside of the body there is a body called the Buddha image,(I call it Astral or Etheric body) the thought which is powerful. The absence of thoughts is Bodhi. The thousand petal lotus flower opens, transformed through breath-energy. (*Crown Chakra?*) Because of the crystallization of the spirit a hundred fold splendour shines forth.' (Aura)

To fulfil Karma, do not give up what comes to you in ordinary life. Give up all thought entanglement of yourself and other people. Think like this and the light within will continue to rotate. The light rotates by itself. Concentrate true thoughts on the space of energy. Different things appear to each person according to their dispositions. If one experiences these things it is a sign of a good aptitude.

You may ask what is enlightenment? I would say it is when you suddenly understand something as a fact of nature and nurture, implicit in a realm where you may or may not exist. It has nothing to do with your understanding or feelings, it is an absolute truth. The living manna of the circulation of the light provides an inner sanctuary within you where the divine light shines. Radiate the divine light within your mind and soul and know that in previous existences you knew all about this divine light within you. Enable the inner light to radiate from within you, rising up through your whole being towards and through the Astral plane and onwards . When the light rotates the Elixir of Life is made spontaneously and the performance of worldly tasks is not a hindrance.

You have heard it said, 'Do unto others as you would have done unto yourself.' But all that you have done unto others you have done unto yourself. If you heal others and make them happy, if you nurture , understand and love them, why not do it for yourself?

These are such dark days with dark deeds being done. But remember that in the dark the light that I speak of shines brightest. No one is pure of sins. So if you can find the mysteries of the light, go on high and inherit the 'Light Kingdom'. It is your due.

Not many believe, but it appears that some holy people can manifest something out of nothing. They know how to work with divine energy. If you believe that this is possible the way is open for you to explore the powers that may lay dormant within you.

Like attracts like and opposites oppose. This is the 'Law of Attraction' within the field of divine magnetism.

No one can absorb all the information in the world and understand all the consequences. The behaviour of the parts is organised by the whole and it is comforting to know that all things are a part of an unbroken web.

On your journey through the 'Great Work' remember to defer to divine will regularly. Your aim should be to progress only as far as has been divinely ordained for you.

You must not attempt to rush the process and if you ask for help or knowledge you must always state; 'providing it is your will God', or 'Thy will be done.' Let me be quite clear here, no progress is good progress without the agreement of the divine light being we call God who controls our life and universe. My understanding is that if you do not believe in a loving God you should not attempt this work as success should always be attributed to divine Astral powers and not down to the physical ego of a person.

Your mind is a time crystal, and as you progress in the work you will see that past, present, and future are equally real to you. Your soul is a time machine that stretches back millions of years. It stretches forward millions of years. You are a time capsule, a time crystal, a lighthouse full of ideas! Let us remind ourselves that the body is only of any interest as an instrument of the soul, and the brain as an instrument for and of the mind.

We are going to spend some time discussing the Astral body now. So, just as our physical body is made of earthly material our Astral body is made up of light from the sun, moon and stars(planets). Humans were created with two forms of vision, firstly they could see that which was equal or lesser than themselves while the light of infused vision permitted them to contemplate that which was greater than mankind.

The Androgyne Sin (the separation from God and of male and female qualities) caused them to lose the second light, leaving them with only corporal vision capable of perceiving only the realm of the material world. Despite this they were able to gain experience of the divine indirectly through the created world. However Ficino tells us in his commentary on 'Corpus Hermetica' that 'the light they still have within draws them to its other half, the infused divine light for which they then long for in the hope of becoming once again whole and they seek their former half in the vision of God.'

Androgyne, the first treatise speaks of the mind who is God being Androgyne and existing as life and light and associated with soul and mind. Humans lost half of themselves, that is God's grace and the wonderful gift of immortality. The light they still have draws them towards it's other half, the infused 'Divine Light' for which they then long for in the hope of once again becoming whole.

Advanced beings who have extraordinary attainment with their higher self can reform the Astral body and hence the physical body of those in need of healing. Since everything physical manifests from the 'Divine Spiritual' this makes complete sense to me and I'm not alone in this belief. Max Heindel takes it a step further when he says; 'It would appear then that our knowledge of the Astral body must be evolved by means of the work of transmutation and will eventually be evolved by humanity as a whole.'

The Astral body, that which we are speaking of, extends to between

16 and 20 inches beyond the physical body. In the past it has been referred to as the 'Philosopher's Stone' by the Medieval Alchemists, the 'Wedding Garment' in the Gospel of St. Matthew and the 'Soul Body' by St. Paul in the First Epistle to the Corinthians. I refer to it as the 'Astral Body' as it has the ability to traverse the Astral dimensions or starry regions.

Now the thought process in the human brain is a tool that mind and intelligence make use of. Thoughts may be fixed or random but it is the art of intelligence that orders them and the conclusions are those which drive our action externally and we then reap their consequences as a result. Even so our free will allows us to choose whether we act or not. Often we act to quickly instead of waiting to see how the matter may resolve itself on its own. The recognition of such activities as strange coincidences act as a marker of realisation for those who have an understanding of divinity and how it may impress itself upon us.

This right quality of mental energy, insight and skill is what I call the art of intelligence and though not everyone necessarily has it within them, all can develop it given the right amount of time and perseverance.

Having a creative flair will enable us sooner or later to meet whatever difficulties arise without getting too lost in the fixity or narrative of categorisation that leads to confusion, despair and failure. In other words, every path can be different but not so different as to warrant failure if personal belief is established from the outset.

So for example, I must think that there is an Astral world before I can see the Astral world. I must want to know more about the Astral world before I start to look for it and I must understand that when I look into what appears to be a void of nothingness or weird and wonderful colours or shapes it will not be very long before my mind starts to attempt to make sense of it.

It will try to form into something familiar to me but I must continue to keep watching it change shape and then attempt to understand how the level of my expectation is driving forward the pattern appearing in front of my eyes. I must monitor my mind and its expectations along with the visions I am having. In this type of meditation the mind must be open to all eventualities but not be led so far down the track that it starts to anticipate what comes next or direct the action as if in a movie.

Faith is a map to follow. Our awareness can only progress if we have faith that there is more to know, that there is something new within us that we have not yet discovered that can make us more than who we are now. I truly believe this marvellous revelation is upon us all now.

The Astral world does not behave like the physical world yet it is clearly connected to it since all life is determined by it, with it, and for it.

When you first start to experience the Astral world you may see only static objects. Some will make sense to you, others perhaps not. After a few times you will probably start to see beings morphing from one animal into another, perhaps even two types of animals joined together. Rather like those from ancient mythology, for example, the Centaur, half horse and half man.

No doubt you will work hard to make sense of what you see but try and remain an independent observer. If you do not your vision may start to cloud over. What you want at that moment is as much clarity as possible. Do not attempt to control the vision in front of you. Just allow it to happen. You will find at a certain time that you will start to move or perhaps fly over many white buildings, square in shape and uniform, some near the coast others inland. You will probably not be able to say what year or time the scene below you represents since you are unlikely to see anything else at this point. On future occasions you may become stationery in the air, or observe from a high point and then, what is below you, may start to move. Sometimes you may even swoop down like a bird to take a closer look, peering in at different angles.

I have been there many times myself. Flying over a coastal town with lots of square white buildings. There were no people . It was night. I said what is the point of me doing this? What is the point of showing me this? I didn't recall getting an answer and have assumed that I should be grateful for the experience, which of course I am . I long realised that there was a reason and it was to show me that I could! Having faith in your teacher helps and knowing that this is all part of the learning experience of many intrepid explorer.

As you progress you will start to see colours, though of a greater brilliance than we see here on earth. Mainly greens and yellows at first then reds and blues but probably not that often and of course everyone's journey is unique for them. So what I described above is not a blueprint, simply an example of what you can expect to occur, a hint at the type of journey you are likely to undertake at the beginning of the 'Great Work'. A journey that we will all be called upon to undertake at some point in our life/lives.

Later you will see many objects, the use of which you may not always understand. But stay with the experience so that your mind has the opportunity to inform further about what you are seeing with your inner or third eye. You will probably witness the unfolding or unwrapping of scenes in front of your eyes and in time you are likely to see some form of Akashic Record. Personally I saw a black box running a black and white film of events that had taken place in World War ll. Exactly what that had to do with me I couldn't say, perhaps nothing at all. But for me that was a very personal experience confirming the existence of the Akashic Record, though I never doubted it.

I believe that God made us primarily as an Astral being. Therefore it is possible to communicate and listen to our Astral mind. Perhaps that is what we are actually doing when we pray. But in terms of everyday living it means we have to learn to switch and tune our physical brain to hear our Astral mind and soul.

We must learn to disregard the background noise of everyday living and of human selfishness and stay focused in true faith that our personal Astral abilities will grow. For that we must learn to nurture ourselves and to love the higher beings.

You may have heard it said; ' That you will know the truth and the truth will set you free.' But what exactly is the truth that will set you free? Well I sincerely hope that my words can be understood by you, and as *Saint Germain* so poetically stated, the knowledge I give you here should be framed in your mind as 'a diamond of lights perfection set in a mounting of perpetual elegance. By perpetual elegance, I mean of course your Astral body made up of a fully connected spirit, mind, and soul.

Remember not everything you see or feel will you understand. Except that this is so. Have much love in your heart and mind but if at any time you start to feel insecure or uncomfortable say a loving prayer and finish the session.

Always take a break and do not feel compelled to proceed when tired. Once the work is started there is no rush to complete because the work is never completed in that sense. You will continue to grow and mature into your own divine self. Whatever plane you are on there will always be more.

Once a tree blossoms and the fruit appears then it rests for a while until it's time to blossom again. The joy of the 'Great Work' is that it never finishes, there is always more to learn. It is like an unending dream landscape with far reaching consequences of happiness.

Understanding our Astral body is paramount . We have spoken a lot about the 'Divine Mind' and your mind, the Divine Light and your light. You have been taught how to see the light within your own being and to see the eye looking back at you in your meditations. So within the pages of this book I hope you will find your truth and that you will be set free from the chains of ignorance that have stopped humanity from evolving ever since the so called 'Fall'.

We are all part of a collective of light and love. Let outer miracles act as evidence of our oneness with each other and of God. The Lord searches all hearts and understands all imaginations of the thoughts.

If you seek you shall find God and God will be found in you.

What you have within you, the light, will save you when you know how to work it. So give birth to what is within you. I have shown you how to expand your inner light but it is you that must do the work. Your inner light should shine all around you. It should shine so that you can see it. Give birth to that which is within you. Expand your inner light. Express your holiness, express your soul, express your Astral being so that others may receive blessings and know themselves and what they have within. The angels and the prophets will come to you and give you what you need.

The Astral plane is spread all across our world but few see it. Likewise the treasure within. Because it is not known to exist it is not searched for.

Though you may seek diligently do not rush the process. Remember it is a two way process. Some work you will do consciously, other work will happen subconsciously.

Seek for your self a day of rest and allow nature to take its course. You are and must remain human even after you have evolved into a being of Astral awareness.

You now know that if you change brainwave frequency through meditation you are able to change your level of consciousness and access to the Astral plane is possible. You know that you will find knowledge that will resonate within you at a deep level. You will become whole.

You know that correct visualisation by the exercise of concentration and will power will enable you to materialise thoughts not only as dreams or visions in the realm of mind but as action and experiences in the material world. You know you are what you think and this is a good way to progress your own evolution. Also by meditating in this manner you happily bring all the various parts of yourself together into one unified powerful and majestic self. You know that visualised images have a potent effect on health and the physical structure of your body.

You know that visualisation and creative prayer can and does alter and reshape the very fabric of one's destiny.

You know that by meditating and venturing deep into the psyche you arrive at an inner world that turns out to envelope, surround or contain that which at first was outer and visible.

You know all of this because you have opened the closed door within your mind. Others did in the past too. They were responsible for building the beautiful churches and magnificent cathedrals, temples and mosques. Long before these were built other ancient monuments were designed and built to verify our respect and knowledge of God and the Astral Plane. Stonehenge and the Pyramids. Egyptian, Indian, Chinese, Greek and other famous temples across the Middle East, Europe and Russia and the rest of the world. Far too many to mention by name, but all telling us the same thing.

The Pantheon built in Rome was designed as a temple for 'All Gods'. Today it is called 'Saint Mary and the Martyrs' and is the burial place of the great artist Raphael, Italian kings and poets. It is a remarkable piece of engineering and design. After nearly 2000 years it remains the largest unsupported dome in the world. The pure beauty is awe inspiring and as if to defy time itself, the light travels anti-clockwise around the dome. It is a spectacular illumination because once the door is shut the Oculus in the centre of the dome is the only source of light. Looking up at the light the worshipper cannot help but feel connected to the Gods. It is reminiscent of the light that we search for when we wish to connect to the Astral plane while searching with our third eye in the temple of our mind. Perhaps the designer said to be *Apollodorus of Damascus* who was commissioned by *Marcus Agrippa*, had exactly this notion in mind when he designed it.

We live in an universe that we are just beginning to understand and it is not out there but within. Reality is established by interaction of consciousness with its environment the visibility of which may or may not be perceived or understood.

We experience existence in this world through our thoughts. Thought comes from mind which is eternal and divine. Since mind does not die we will continue to experience existence long after physical death. That is why I say we do not die.

Knowledge and our developed personality are two things we will take with us into the future after we have physically left our body.

Before, at, or after, we leave our body we will realise that we are still the same soul. We will realise that it is not the material things of life that matter but the memory of the joys and sorrows and shared experiences that serve as real growth and nourishment for our future self. We are literally the maker of our own soul.

Importantly how we see the world is how we will continue to see our surroundings. Our surroundings and how we feel will be painted upon the scenery that we move into. That is why we should do everything out of love. While we live, love as much as we can. It will always be repaid. Gain as much knowledge as we can especially knowledge related to self growth and the knowledge that helps us to help others wherever and whenever we can.

We know that the ability to visualise and create is possible with specific training here on the earth plane. Once learnt it will serve us well on the Astral plane. We must learn to visualise our preferred destination, our desired creation, not just for our sake but for the sake of all God's beings. We know that creative work requires a creative mind. We are open to all possibilities without preconceived ideas.

Be ready to see something new. Have a passionate desire but do not order. Instead observe and wonder if you want to learn how the Astral plane works. As a person desires, so their destiny. You will be surrounded by other beings , some more powerful and others less so. Some things you will understand and others you will need help with. It is the same for all of us.

That is why it is important to love and come to peace with all that is around you. It is not only because you share a future together or that you are very much part of all you experience here on Earth, but when you leave the body you are to partake in a partly self made existence that has roots on the material and Astral plane and remember you will not be alone!

It is believed that the only judgement that takes place is self judgement. This arises solely out of one's own feelings of guilt and repentance. Love is the key and if we can develop this passion with copious amounts of empathy and conquer personal ego we will do very well indeed.

One out of every five people will more than likely have an out of body experience (OOB) at sometime in their life. As we experience new wonders, our abilities start to grow and we learn to become more intrepid and gradually lose our fears. I have said this is not a programme that can be rushed. Everyone's journey is different. Out of Body travellers can see in all directions at once. Some can see through their skin. A blind girl could see through the tip of her nose. A Russian woman could apparently read through her fingertips.

Though our lives are planned out to some extent we each play a role in the creation of this life plan.

Our material reality is a slower version of the afterlife dimension and frequency. It takes more time for our beliefs or wishes to re sculpt our bodies into things such as stigmata and for the symbolic language of our psyches to manifest externally as synchronicities, or as we see it , coincidences, but manifest they do.

We have all experienced strange coincidences in our life and many times we have even commented upon them. When we come to watch and listen what is actually happening to us in our life we come to realise that there is a teacher present within us guiding our experiences and watching over us. We must learn how to communicate with our teacher.

When the Two Become One

When two become one
The inner person and the outer person
The soul and the body
The brain and the mind
The mind and heart
The soul and the mind
When they all become one
The outer sun and the inner sun
The inner world and the outer world
When the two become one
The one that heals and the one that is healed
The one that gives and the one that is given
The one that loves and the one that is loved
When the two become one
When the rich in spirit become the spirit that is rich
When the poor become wealthy and the wealthy become poorer
When the two become one,

When the male becomes female and the female male
When the outside becomes inside and the inside turns outside
Then the two become one
When those that take begin to give
And those that give learn to take
Then the two become one and
That which is above appears below
When the soul and the spirit unite in love
All this in the name of the enlightened one
That lives forever, who is always our protector
And is the beginning and the end
The alpha and omega

New

Be a new human of a new Earth
One who takes and one who gives
You are an ocean in which all fish swim
You are the air through which all birds fly
You are the earth from which sprout the trees
Be a new human of a new Earth
One who takes and one who gives.
Where the beginning is so is the end.
If you know the beginning then you will know
That death of the soul does not exist

Emanuel Swedenborg (1688-1772) was a Swedish Lutheran theologian and philosopher. He was also a scientist writer and philosopher and famous mystic. On opening the 'Book of Lives' Swedenborg explains, A person's life review occurs when they die. This is possible because the information was recorded in the nervous system of the person's spiritual body, Thus in order to evoke the life review an angel has to examine the individual's entire body beginning with the fingers of each hand and proceeding through the whole.

Swedenborg refers to thought balls that the angels use to communicate and says they are no different from the portrayals he could see in the wave substance that surrounded a person (Aura, Astral body). He describes these telepathic bursts of knowledge as a picture language so dense with information that each image contains a thousand ideas. A communicated series that can last several hours in such a sequential arrangement that one can only marvel. (Similar perhaps to the Akashic Record) In additions to using portrayals angels also employ a speech that contains concepts that are beyond human understanding.

In fact the main reason they use portrayals is because it is the only way they can make even a pale version of their thoughts and ideas comprehensible to human beings. Swedenborg said that he was astonished to find that in heaven there are also spirits from other planets, an astounding assertion for a man born over three hundred years ago.

Despite its ghostlike and ephemeral qualities heaven is actually a more fundamental level of reality than our own physical world. It is the archetypal source from which all earthly forms originate and to which all forms return. All things in physical reality arise from this spiritual reality.

Each of us is a heaven in miniature and underlying visible reality is a wave-like substance (Ether?) from which our universe is constantly being created. There are at least two waves. According to Swedenborg one comes from us, our soul, and the other from heaven.

The idea that subtle levels of reality can be accessed through a shift in consciousness alone is one of the main premises of the Yogic tradition. The material world is a frozen version of the thought built reality of heaven. The matter that makes up both heaven and earth flows in stages from the Divine and at each new stage it becomes more general and therefore courser and hazier and it becomes slower and therefore more viscous and colder.

Most people possess a mental screen that keeps them from seeing beyond the veil of matter but when one learns to peer beyond this veil one finds that everything is compiled of different intensities of luminous vibrations.

The feeling of having electrical currents running through parts or all of your body is a common high-energy sensation that is experienced in the vibrational state of awareness prior to you having an out of body experience. I have travelled and personally experienced this phenomena many times.

As already mentioned *Robert Monroe* was an expert and has written books on the subject. He also founded The Monroe Institute. In my opinion he is worthy of attention. Robert said ‘ Perhaps the second body (what I call the Astral or Etheric body) in that second state can provide the quantum jump to prove God empirically’.

Robert makes reference to one of his experiences where he describes observing a 'Divine Being'. 'As he passes there is a roaring musical sound and a feeling of a radiant irresistible force of ultimate power that peaks overhead.'

I can verify that sensation as I have had similar experiences that confirm what he says.

Naturally we are all afraid initially to have an 'Out of Body Experience'. But the feeling is the same as when you first learn to swim. You are naturally afraid of the water until you have mastered the art of swimming. It is the same for Astral plane travel. You cannot be comfortable until you do it and see there is nothing more to fear on the Astral plane than there is on the physical or material plane.

Michael Talbot in his book, The Holographic Universe; page 262; cites an interesting passage about *Swami Sri Yukteswar Giri* , He was a Hindu holy man who said he could pass back and forth between this world and the next and described the afterlife dimension as a world composed of various subtle vibrations of light and colour and hundreds of times larger that the material cosmos. 'It is infinitely more beautiful than our own realm of existence and abounded with opal lakes, bright seas and rainbow rivers. Because it is more vibrant with Gods creative light, it's weather is always pleasant and it's only climatic manifestations are occasional falls of luminous white snow and rain of many coloured lights'.

He goes on to say that 'Individuals can manifest any body they want and can see with any area of their body. They can also materialize any fruit or food they desire and feast only on the ambrosia of eternally new knowledge.'

'They communicate through a telepathic series of light pictures and rejoice at the immortality of friendship and the indestructibility of love. They also feel keen pain if any mistake is made in the conduct or perception of truth and when they are confronted with a multitude of relatives, fathers, mothers, wives, husbands and friends acquired during their various incarnations on Earth, they are at a loss as to whom to love especially and thus learn to give a divine and equal love to all.'

To explore the new country we must first learn to leave the old one behind. *Sri Aurobindo* explains there is a realm beyond space and time composed of multi coloured infinity of vibrations peopled by non-physical beings. (out of body souls) They are so far in advance of human consciousness that they make us look like children. They take any form of being they choose in order to make themselves more accessible to a particular consciousness. In their truest forms they appear as vibrations. Information can be gathered by a single glance. Sri Aurobindo also claimed that all matter has some degree of consciousness. ' If all matter were not conscious no Yogi could move an object with his mind because there would be no possibility of contact between the Yogi and the object.'

It is only as we descended from the higher vibrational levels of reality to the lower that a progressive law of fragmentation took place leaving us bereft of the powers we once had. The proof that we have arrived at a low level of existence is the fragmentation we see all around that is destroying us and our environment. To make a real difference to our environment here on planet Earth we have to learn to make the jump up onto a higher vibrational frequency ourselves while in this physical body. Only that way will humanity evolve onto the higher planes of existence where we were before the so called fall. This fragmentation causes all wars on the planet and of course it has led to the concept of death. The concept that when we age and finally pass out of this body we are dead and that is the end of it! As a result we feel we have to do all our living, loving, and hating along with our eating, acquiring, and enjoyment within a certain rushed time frame. As soon as we realise that we go on and our minds and soul do not die, the time frame changes and we can start to relax.

Suddenly we begin to feel different within ourselves and it is this difference within our inner core that then starts to drive the mental exploration of our mind and the Astral plane. There is no doubt that we are following a path of spiritual evolution where the learning never stops. This is what this book has been about. We like to think of ourselves as being a highly civilised and sophisticated society with amazing technological feats and it is true we have done well on this front. But there is so much more we can and must do.

We can take our lead from the magnificent Yogis and Masters of religion who taught us that there is a better life to be had. Ask your Mother and Father in heaven to tell you everything and to explain the great secret that I speak of in the pages of this book.

I know we live in a world where thoughts are everything, poison or perfection, but as I have said many times we also need to listen to the wellsprings of our heart. In our hearts we want to know and that desire never leaves us. That is why I encourage you to listen to your heart. The true meaning of power is virtue, self control and truth.

The only constancy in our work is non constancy! Our souls do not speak in words all the time.

'From the time of the awareness of the existence of the soul until the resolution of the apocalyptic potential, there are roughly fifty thousand years, We are now, there can be no doubt, in the final historical seconds of that crisis. A crisis which involves the end of history, our departure from the planet and the triumph over death. We are in fact closing the distance with the most profound event a planetary ecology can encounter, the freeing of life from the dark chrysalis of matter .' *Terence McKenna*

Clearly the signs are there. We are following our own tracks of spiritual evolution. The learning process never stops. Sometimes we are allowed glimpses of the higher planes. Each one is lighter and brighter than the one before. Our abilities will always demand more!

In this new found existence one may apply known ideas to new contexts and conversely new contexts to known ideas!

Generally speaking there is no reason to expect that any given set of natural laws will have an unlimited domain of validity. Everything is possible yet presumably as far as one can see , on any given plain of reality there will be fixed laws.

I personally believe that there are eternal truths that are divine profound and perpetual.

Creative work requires a creative state of mind a non conformist state that accepts anything goes!

This is the time of big separation and in this time we become what we believe. Well I don't believe in separation but unity. That means I don't believe in personal opinion in as much as it only serves me! The greater good must be served if we are to survive.

We will come to understand that the out of body experience is as normal as the experience of being in the body. After all when you go to sleep you do not know what you are going to dream or indeed that you are going to have a dream, yet dream you do! And as you fall to sleep you can feel that frequency upload or lift that takes you to a place where everything is everything. Time and space cease to exist in the world beyond but you know that you are still you. The world beyond is suffused with a light more brilliant than any you have seen on Earth. Do not draw a rigid boundary between being awake, sleeping or dreaming. What happens to you in a dream is part of your soul's experience and reality. Knowledge will come to you from many places. From your dreams, from other humans, from plants and animals and even stones communicate to our souls, for within our souls these things exist and our mind knows it.

When we are out of body the vista is made up of many things we do not understand that is why we must learn to see beyond our made up mind and reach out into infinity bravely. We can ask for help and we should do so more often. Sometimes we see glimpses of the higher planes, each one is lighter and brighter than the one before. There are many higher planes and to get back to God, to reach the plane where the Divine Spirit lives we have to learn to drop our outer garment each time until our Spirit is truly free.

Like Joseph and his multicoloured coat we have many outer garments to transform and we do this through the so called death process. But mark me well and make no mistake, we are who we are and we know who we are all through this process of self realisation.

Now it is possible that this uncovering of our blatant soul of so many lives is where we will have the greatest difficulty of acceptance. It is perhaps, the hardest thing that we will ever have to do. To acknowledge who we really are because we will no longer just be the person of this one life, but the person of many lives. The person, the soul, the mind that did not die and who is, even as I write now, gathering experience, knowledge and love into their magnificent Astral being.

May all your new experiences bring a blessing upon you and those you know.

Lucy Caxton Brown
26th December 2018

Further Reading

Active Consciousness, Awakening The Power Within; Amy L. Lansky, Ph.D 2003 R.L. Ranch Press

Anaxagoras And Universal Mind; Richard Geldard, 2007 Ralph Waldo Emerson Books

Aristotle; The Metaphysics; Translated with an Introduction by Hugh Lawson-Tancred; Penguin Books

Astral Projection; the definitive survey on Out -Of- Body Experiences ; 1929 Dr. Robert Crookall B.Sc (Psychology) D.Sc., Ph.D. Citadel Press

Awakening The Mind, A Guide To Mastering The Power Of Your Brain Waves; Anna Wise; Jeremy P. Tarcher/Putnam,

Awakening Your Psychic Powers; An Edgar Cayce Guide, Henry Reed, Ph.D. 1988, St Martin's Press

A Suggestive Inquiry Into The Hermetic Mystery; Mary Anne Atwood, 2013 Reprint Isha Books

Corpus Hermetica; 1471 Translated by Marcilio Ficino

Dreams of a Spirit Seer; Emanuel Swedenborg, 1766 Translated by Immanuel Kant; Swedenborg Foundation

Early Magnetism in its Higher Relations to Humanity; Thomas South 1846 H. Bailliere Publisher London.

Edgar Cayce on the Spiritual Forces Within You; John Van Auken, 2014 A.R.E. Press

How To Know Higher Worlds; Rudolf Steiner,1994 Anthroposophic Press Inc.

Iamblicus; On the Mysteries 300 A.D.

Journeys Out Of The Body; Robert A. Monroe , 1972 Souvenir Press

Light On The Path; Through The Gates Of Gold. Mabel Collins 1997 Theosophical University Press;

Modern Miracles; An Investigative Report On Psychic Phenomena Associated With Sathya Sai Baba; Erlendur Haraldsson, Ph.D 1988 Ballantine Books

Saint German; Studies In Alchemy, The Science of Self-Transformation; Dictated to the Messenger Mark. L Prophet , 1962. Summit University Press

On Creativity; David Bohm, 1996, Routledge Classics

Out-Of -Body Experiences; A Fourth Analysis ;Robert Crookall

B.Sc. (Psychology) D.Sc.,1970, University Books Inc.
Paracelsus; Treasured Hermetic And Alchemical Writings;Translated By A.E. White 2009, A Cornerstone Book
Pistis Sophia; A Gnostic Gospel ; G.R.S. Mead, 1921, J.M.Watkins London
Signatura Rerum; Jacob Boehme 2011 Aziloth Books
The Emerald Tablet; (Smaragdine Tablet) Hermes Trismegistus
The Holographic Universe; Michael Talbot , 1996, Harper Collins Publishers
The Key Of Jacob Boehme; Translated by William Law, 1991 Phanes Press
Selected Works of Plotinus; 1914 Translated by Thomas Taylor, G Bell and Sons Ltd
The Stages of Higher Knowledge; Rudolf Steiner;1967, Anthroposophic Press Inc
The Secret of the Soul; William Buhlman, 2001 Harper Collins
The Secret Teachings Of All Ages; Manly P. Hall; 1928, Wildside Press LLC.
Ultimate Journey; Robert A. Monroe ,1994 Doubleday
Vibrational Medicine; Richard Gerber;1988 Bear and Co

Books By Lucy Caxton Brown

FOXED; For Those Who Want To Know The Truth

Alexander; A New Theory On An Ancient Legend

The Amber Queen

The Small Book Of Poems Including Golden Ray and Cupids Child

The River Centaur

Romany Voices

The Wildfire Dragon

Diamond Mind

The Key

Castle In The Sky And Other Selected Poems

www.ingramcontent.com/pod-product-compliance
Ingram Content Group UK Ltd.
Pitfield, Milton Keynes, MK11 3LW, UK
UKHW041642190726
13854UKWH00006B/2647

9 781789 554465